KURSK 1943
LAST GERMAN OFFENSIVE IN THE EAST

C CASEMATE | ILLUSTRATED

KURSK 1943
LAST GERMAN OFFENSIVE IN THE EAST

IAN BAXTER

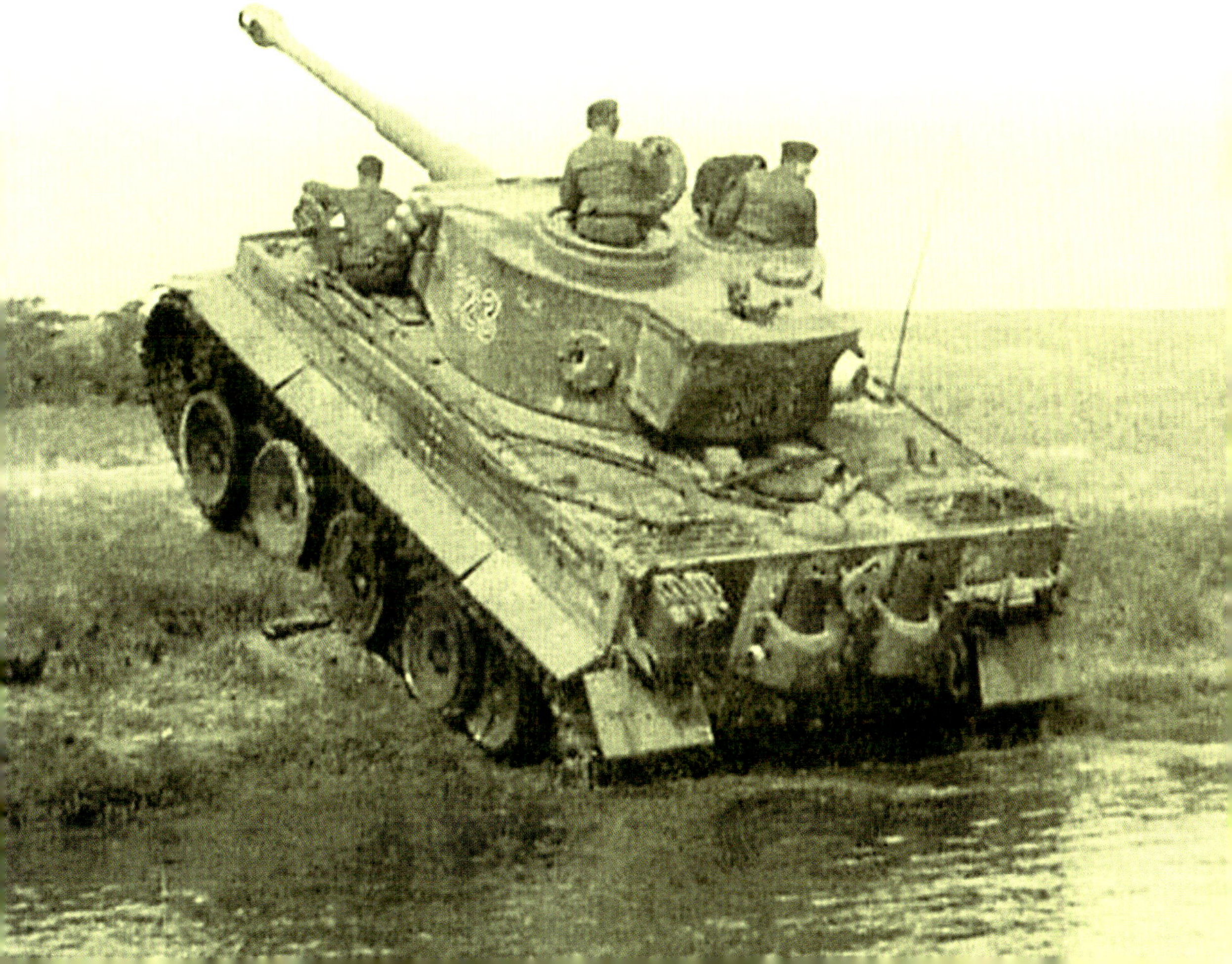

CASEMATE | ILLUSTRATED

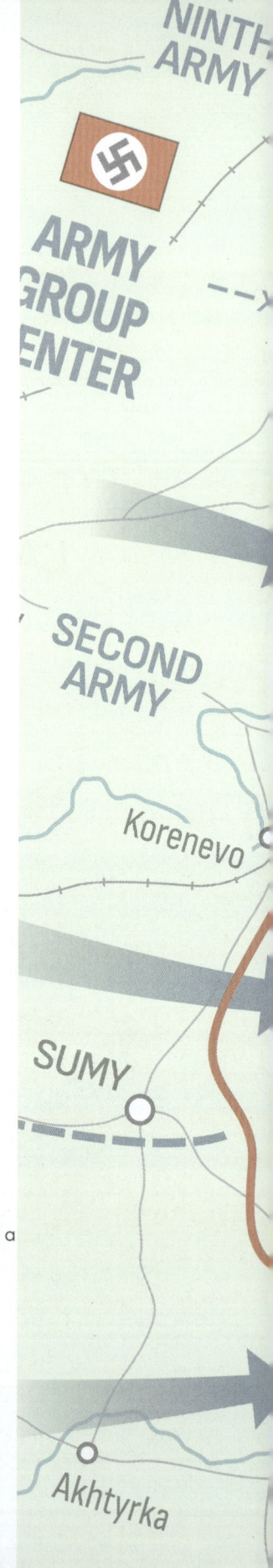

CIS0014

Print Edition: ISBN 978-1-61200-7076
Digital Edition: ISBN 978-1-61200-7083

© Casemate Publishers 2019

All rights reserved. No part of this book may be reproduced or transmitted in any form or by any means, electronic or mechanical including photocopying, recording or by any information storage and retrieval system, without permission from the publisher in writing.

Design by Battlefield Design
Color profiles by Tom Cooper
Printed and bound by Megaprint, Turkey

CASEMATE PUBLISHERS (US)
Telephone (610) 853-9131
Fax (610) 853-9146
Email: casemate@casematepublishers.com
www.casematepublishers.com

CASEMATE PUBLISHERS (UK)
Telephone (01865) 241249
Fax (01865) 794449
Email: casemate-uk@casematepublishers.co.uk
www.casematepublishers.co.uk

Title page: Tiger tank belonging to the *schwere Panzer Abteilung 503* negotiates a river prior to operations at Kursk.
Contents page: A StuG.III advancing across a field. From 1943 until the end of the war the assault guns were slowly absorbed into the panzer and panzergrenadier divisions of the Wehrmacht and Waffen-SS.
Map: The German front line and the planned drive of Army Groups Center and North against the Red Army Western, Bryansk, Central, Steppe, and Voronezh Fronts on July 5, 1943.

Note: vehicle illustrations and profiles are not to scale.

Contents

Timeline of Events 6
Prelude to Disaster 8
The Opposing Forces 14
Soviet Preparations for Battle 22
German Preparations for Battle 34
Army Group Center 56
Army Group South 88
Aftermath 122
Further Reading 126
Index 127

Timeline of Events

The battle of Kursk in July 1943 was the final strategic offensive that the Germans were able to launch on the Eastern Front. The codename for the offensive, Operation *Zitadelle* (*Citadel*), was an attack aimed at a double envelopment concentrated on Kursk with the sole intention of surrounding the Red Army forces of five armies and closing off the salient. For this historic attack the Germans committed two army groups: Army Group Center, which was to form a northern pincer, and Army Group South, which would launch its powerful panzer divisions, including the crème of the Waffen-SS, against the southern face of the salient.

May 1943

For several weeks prior to the offensive, whilst the Soviets prepare their defenses, the Germans use this period for training and rehearsals, and building their arsenal in the Kursk region. Panzer units are replenished with men and equipment: the German force soon boasts 12 panzer and five panzergrenadier divisions.

June 1943

During the final weeks leading up to the battle, German units are moved to their jump-off points, armored regiments are unloaded from trains and redirected to their combat zones, and final preparations are meticulously put in place by the German high command. The Red Army are also finalizing their defensive arcs which comprise various antitank strongpoints, artillery, heavy and light machine gun positions and independent tank and self-propelled gun brigades, and regiments tasked with the infantry counterattacks.

A Wehrmacht reconnaissance motorcycle unit passes two destroyed Soviet tanks during the early phase of the battle

Timeline of Events

An SS soldier from Das Reich in his summer camouflage smock on the advance to Kursk. Behind him are Das Reich Tiger tanks.

July 5, 1943 Following a massive artillery bombardment, Army Group Center and Army Group South launch their attack against the Kursk salient. It does not take long before a combination of fierce resistance, minefields, thick mud and mechanical breakdowns begin taking their toll. However, in spite of this, the first day progresses relatively well with a number of breakthroughs along the front.

July 6, 1943 Whilst the two German army groups continue to push forward, the Soviet Central Front counterattacks. Although the offensive fails, it is enough to grind down the German Ninth Army, which has only gained some six miles of ground in 24 hours.

July 11, 1943 Army Group South launches its great attack toward Prokhorovka meeting stiff resistance from tank and infantry units of the Soviet Voronezh Front.

July 12, 1943 The battle of Prokhorovka erupts when 500 tanks of Rotmistrov's 5th Guards Tank Army attack the II Panzer Corps in what becomes one of the largest tank battles in history.

July 13, 1943 Following the battle of Prokhorovka, which sees the combined loss of some 700 German and Soviet tanks, the II Panzer Corps is unable to make further progress, with poor ground conditions hampering resupply. The Red Army drives back the 3rd Panzer Division in the Rakovo–Kruglik area and recaptures the town of Berezovka. Hitler calls off *Zitadelle*, and what follows is a massive Soviet offensive against the Orel bulge.

JULY 1943

July 7, 1943 Hoth's Fourth Panzer Army makes a number of deep penetrations into the salient and covers some 20 miles, coming to within striking distance of Pokrovka.

July 8, 1943 Although the Red Army retakes the city of Kursk, reports confirm that in Army Group South, the SS Panzer Corps are involved in a number of successful engagements: Totenkopf has smashed its way through more than 30 miles of Russian lines, whilst the Leibstandarte and Das Reich are proving equally successful.

July 9, 1943 Hoth launches an attack with more than 500 tanks along a 10-mile front between Verkhopenye and Solotino. Within a few hours the panzers, at great cost, are within just 12 miles of Oboyan. Hoth regroups and shifts his axis of advance northeastward toward Prokhorovka.

July 10, 1943 By July 10, Model's Ninth Army has little chance of reaching Kursk. After five long days of almost continuous combat, the German troops are exhausted and in places fighting for survival. Model's situation has become desperate. However, his panzer and panzergrenadier divisions continue the assault on Ponyri.

July 14, 1943 Whilst panzer and panzergrendier units either try to maintain their positions or begin a slow withdrawal, the Waffen-SS begins the final operation in the Kursk salient before pulling out. Totenkopf is forced from its bridgehead on the northern bank of the Psel River, while, farther east, Das Reich has made limited progress in capturing the town of Belenichino. The Grossdeutschland Division is ordered to attack westward, in order to recapture the ground lost by the 3rd Panzer Division.

July 15, 1943 Das Reich makes contact with the 7th Panzer Division. However, the Soviet offensive to the north of the salient now threatens the Ninth Army's rear and it is forced to begin a withdrawal westward to avoid encirclement. All offensive action around Prokhorovka ceases and German forces in the area go over to the defensive. Hitler orders the SS Panzer Corps out of the salient.

A whitewashed Tiger tank moving towards the front during winter operations on the Eastern Front in 1943.

| Prelude to Disaster

The battle of Kursk was to become the largest tank battle of World War II. During this ferocious clash of arms the Red Army would savagely contest every foot of ground, and finally end German invincibility forever. For the first time in its short history, the blitzkrieg concept would fail.

By May 1942, following the German armies' stagnation along the entire Eastern Front, there was renewed confidence among the German high command. Tank production had increased with more panzer divisions being raised, and motorized divisions converted into panzergrenadier divisions. Although equipping the Heer's Panzerwaffe was a slow, expensive process, it was undertaken effectively with the introduction of a number of new, fresh divisions being deployed on the front lines.

With the Panzerwaffe now fully equipped for battle, a new offensive was unleashed in southern Russia, codenamed Operation *Fall Blau* (*Case Blue*). Some 15 panzer divisions and panzergrenadier divisions of the First and Fourth Armies, together with Italian, Rumanian, and Hungarian formations, crashed into action. In just two days the spearheads had

Prelude to Disaster

A column of Pz.Kpfw.IVs roll across a field during winter operations in southern Russia in early 1943. The Pz.Kpfw.IV had become the workhorse of the Panzerwaffe, having distinguished itself on the battlefield with much success.

penetrated 100 miles deep into the enemy lines and began to cut off the city of Voronezh. The city fell on July 7. The two panzer armies then converged with all their combined might on Stalingrad. It seemed that the Russians were now doomed and so Hitler decided to abandon the armored advance on Stalingrad and embark on an encirclement operation down on the Don. The Sixth Army was to go on and capture Stalingrad without any real panzer support and fight a bloody battle of attrition there. Eventually the fighting became so fierce it embroiled some 21 German divisions including six panzer and panzergrenadier divisions.

The Sixth Army soon became encircled and three hurriedly reorganized, understrength panzer divisions were thrown into a relief operation. By December 19, the 6th Panzer Division had fought its way to within 35 miles of Stalingrad. But under increasing Soviet pressure the relief operation failed. The 6th Panzer

Panzergrendiers on the move. By March 1943 the Wehrmacht had more or less wrenched back the strategic initiative on the Eastern Front, on both the southern and central fronts. Infantry reserves were now trickling through to support the front and the badly depleted panzers divisions were being replenished.

A Marder II panzerjäger. Some 185 of these vehicles were converted on Pz.Kpfw.II Ausf.D and E variants and an additional 50 Ausf.F models were introduced during the summer of 1942. They were a popular interim solution in antitank warfare and much needed by the mid-war period against growing enemy resistance.

A Pz.Kpw.IV knocked out of action during the third battle of Kharkov in March 1943. The German victory at Kharkov infused confidence into the German high command and was another contributing factor to Hitler's determination to unleash a large offensive in the area by the summer of that year.

Division and remnants of the Fourth Panzer Army were forced to retreat, leaving the Sixth Army in the encircled city to its fate. Some 94,000 soldiers surrendered on February 2, 1943. With them the 14th, 16th, and 24th Panzer Divisions, and the 3rd, 29th, and 60th Panzergrenadier Divisions were annihilated.

Following the loss of Stalingrad at the end of January 1943, German Army Group South was desperately trying to hold its receding front. However, many units had already fallen back in disorganized retreat across the southern Ukraine. As further problems beset the German forces in the snow, the Soviet high command, the Stavka, had decided to unleash the third and final stage of Operation *Little Saturn*, which they hoped would drive the Germans out of the Ukraine forever. This ambitious operation committed the Voronezh Front to the offensive.

Under massive artillery bombardment and armored attack, it was reported that Kursk and Belgorod fell on February 9, 1943. German reconnaissance then monitored Soviet forces simultaneously advancing west from the Donetz bend around Isyum. In the gap between the Dnieper and the right wing of Army Group Center, there was practically nothing to defend Army Detachment Lanz and Army Group B's badly battered Second Army west of Kursk. As a consequence, the Russians pushed farther west and captured Kharkov on February 16, threatening the German defenses in the city of Rostov.

Troops march through a captured Russian city in March 1943. In the background, a Pz.Kpfw.IV can be seen supporting the advance. Whilst many parts of the front had stagnated, in the south and the Ukraine, the campaign was being decided. Exhausted Soviet forces had begun a slow retreat eastward and the city of Kharkov was recaptured. As a direct result of this success, plans were immediately drawn up for a massive offensive in the Kursk salient.

Waffen-SS troops wearing their distinctive anorak winter jackets during a pause in fighting in 1943. For the Kursk offensive Hitler would instruct the cream of the Waffen-SS to spearhead the attack.

German armor, including Pz.Kpfw.IVs, on the move during an operation in the spring of 1943. Within weeks of this photograph much of this armor would be directed to the Kursk region to prepare for a summer offensive.

What followed in the last two weeks of February was a tenacious German defense, which consequently saw only minor Russian gains made west of Kursk, and none at all at Orel. Hitler and Field Marshal Erich von Manstein were fully aware that the winter battles had left Army Group Don battered, but their German resilience persisted. Several panzer units had enough strength to launch a number of counterattacks and Manstein's counteroffensive was stiffened by an SS panzer corps equipped with Tiger tanks. On February 20, Manstein fought his way from Poltava back toward Kharkov, thus gaining the initiative between the Donetz and Dnieper rivers. It appeared that Manstein had finally restored the army group's position in southern Russia.

In Army Group Center too, the front lines had also been stabilized. Along hundreds of miles of the front a mass of minefields, trenches, bunkers, and antitank-gun and machine-gun emplacements had been built. The well-constructed road network too allowed the rapid movement of reinforcements to the area. Over a period of three months these strong defensive lines were attacked by the Russians who made a series of coordinated assaults in the Kursk and northern Army Group Center areas with the ultimate objective of encircling the entire army group. However, the Red Army had overestimated the strength and resilience of the German forces in Army Group Center and eventually the Soviet attacks from Kursk toward Orel petered out. As a result the offensive was called off.

By March Army Group Center had maintained, more or less, the strategic initiative on the Eastern Front. With infantry reserves now slowly coming through to support the front and with the buildup and transformation of the badly depleted panzers divisions improving, confidence within the German high command once more returned.

On a training ground in the spring of 1943 are new Panther tanks prior to being sent to Kursk in late June to see combat for the first time.

| The Opposing Forces

The German soldier on the Eastern Front in 1943 was transformed from the man he had been in June 1941. He had endured almost ceaseless fighting against a growing, ferocious enemy that was persistently and vigorously defending and attacking. Now, he was armed with more powerful, uparmored weapons to deal with the developing threat in order to try and restore his precarious situation.

The German Soldier in 1943

The opening months of 1943 for the German soldiers on the Eastern Front were very gloomy. They had fought desperately to maintain cohesion and hold their positions during battles that often saw thousands perish. By the end of January Stalingrad had been lost, which consequently allowed the Soviets to open a second offensive, codenamed Operation *Star*, with the cities of Belgorod, Kursk, and Kharkov as its objectives.

What followed under Manstein's command was to instruct the Wehrmacht to try and restore the front in southern Russia, which allowed Hitler to plan a new offensive on the Eastern Front. By March it was clear that this new offensive would be in the Kursk region with the objective being a rapid and concentrated attack by shock armies from the Belgorod area and south of Orel to annihilate the enemy.

However, by May the German soldier was aware he had been severely weakened by the overwhelming strength of the Red Army. To make matters worse, during the first half of 1943 troop units had not been refitted with substantial replacements to compensate for the large losses sustained. Supplies of equipment, too, were often insufficient in some areas of the front and there was a quiet realization that they were now fighting an enemy who was often far superior to them, and with an inexhaustible supply of reinforcements. As a consequence, in a number of sectors of the front soldiers were able to realistically assess the situation and this in turn managed to save the lives of many who would have normally been killed fighting to the last man. In spite of the adverse situation in which the German soldier was placed during the first half of 1943, he was still strong, determined to fight with courage and skill.

By June the German forces had expended considerable combat effort through lack of sufficient reconnaissance and the necessary support of tanks and heavy weapons, and yet the German war machine was still able to rearm for a massive offensive in the Kursk region, gambling virtually the whole of the Panzerwaffe in one single battle. This was in stark contrast to the fact that in many sectors of the front the Red Army was constantly outgunning the Wehrmacht. In spite of this, German soldiers in their thousands were directed to the German Central Front to build up their forces for the coming offensive.

The German Soldier's Personal Equipment and Weapons

Adolf Hitler with his generals.

The German soldier was still very well equipped by 1943. The rifleman, or *schütze*, wore the trademark model 1935 steel helmet, which provided ample protection whilst marching to the front and during combat. His leather belt with support straps carried two sets of three ammunition pouches for a total of 60 rounds for his carbine. The soldier also wore his combat harness for his mess kit and special camouflage rain cape or *zeltbahn*. He carried an entrenching tool, and attached to the entrenching tool carrier was the bayonet, a bread bag for rations, gasmask canister, which was invariably slung over the wearer's shoulder and an anti-gas cape in its pouch attached to the shoulder strap. The infantryman's flashlight was normally attached to the tunic and inside the tunic pocket he carried wound dressings. A small backpack was issued, though some did not wear them. The backpack was intended for spare clothing, personal items, and additional rations along with a spare clothing satchel.

The weapons used by the German soldier varied, but the standard issue piece of equipment was the 7.92mm Kar98k carbine. This excellent modern and effective bolt-action rifle was of Mauser design. This rifle remained the most popular weapon used by the German Army throughout the war. Another weapon used by the German Army, but not to the extent of the Kar98k, was the 9mm MP38 or MP40 machine pistol. This submachine gun was undoubtedly one of the most effective weapons ever produced for the German war machine.

The 7.92mm MG34 light machine gun was yet another weapon that featured heavily within the ranks of the German Army. The effectiveness of this weapon made it the most superior machine gun produced at that time. The MG34 and later the MG42 possessed impressive rates of fire and could dominate the battlefield both in defensive and offensive roles. The German Army possessed the MG34 in every rifle group, and machine-gun crews were able to easily transport this relatively light weapon onto the battlefield by resting it over the shoulder. Yet another weapon, which was seen at both company and battalion

A photograph showing the uniform worn by a *panzerjäger* officer. The uniform was specially designed primarily to be worn inside and away from armored vehicles, and for this reason designers produced a garment that gave better camouflage qualities than the standard black panzer uniform.

level on the battlefield, was the 5cm l.GrW36 light mortar and 8cm s. GrW34 heavy mortar. Although they could both be effective weapons when fired accurately, the heavy mortar was far too heavy and too expensive to be produced on a large scale.

At regimental and divisional level the Heer possessed its own artillery in the form of 7.5cm lIG 18, 10.5cm lFH 18, 15cm sFH 18, and 15cm sIG 33 infantry guns. Specially trained artillery crews manned these guns, which were seen extensively until the mid-war in 1943.

German Armored Crew

Throughout the war on the Eastern Front, the armored crews, or *panzertruppen*, fought with courage and determination and earned a formidable reputation for their skill and tenacity on the battlefield. Wearing their special black panzer uniforms, the panzertruppen were easily distinguished from the German soldier in his field-gray service uniform. The color of the uniform was specially dyed in black purely to hide oil and other stains from the environment of working with armored vehicles. The black uniform was also a traditional color used by the legendary Prussian 5th and 9th Hussar Regiments of Fredrick the Great's army in the mid-18th century. The elite Life Guard Hussars of the Napoleonic-era Prussian and Imperial German armies also wore black. The cap badge worn by the 5th and later the Life Hussars was the famous *totenkopf*, or death's head, badge, which became synonymous with the panzer arm during the war. Now, over a century later Hitler's elite German armored troops were wearing black uniforms that had incorporated similar designs to the elite forces of the once-vaunted Prussian and Imperial German forces. Across the vastness of Russia these black uniforms symbolized a band of elite troops, the Wehrmacht spearhead with their armored vehicles, who gained the greatest fame, or notoriety, as part of the all-powerful panzer divisions.

The black panzer uniform itself was made of high-quality black wool, which was smooth and free of imperfections. The uniform comprised a short black double-breasted jacket worn with loose-fitting black trousers. The deep double-breasted jacket was high waisted and specially designed to allow the wearer to move around inside his cramped vehicle with relative comfort. The trousers were also designed to be loose in order to allow the wearer plenty of movement.

The headgear still worn by many panzermen in mid-1943 was the field cap, or *feldmütze*, which was identical to the design and shape of the army officer's field cap, and was worn by all ranks. It was black and had the national emblem stitched in white on the front on the cap above a woven cockade, which was displayed in the national colors. However, in 1943, just prior to Kursk, a new form of headdress was introduced, the *einheitsfeldmütze*, better known as the enlisted panzerman's model 1943 field cap. The M1943 cap was issued in black, but when stocks ran low troops were seen wearing field-gray field caps. Both colors of the design were worn universally among panzer crews and the cap insignia differed only slightly between the various ranks.

The field-gray Wehrmacht steel helmet was also issued to the *panzertruppen* as part of their regulation uniform. Generally, the steel helmet was not worn inside the cramped confines of a tank, except when crossing over rough terrain and normally when the crewmember was exposed under combat conditions outside his vehicle. Many crews, however, utilized their steel helmets as added armored protection and attached them to the side of the tank's cupola, and to the rear of the vehicle.

Another item of headgear worn by the panzer arm was the officer's service cap, or *schirmmütze*. The cap was identical to the Heer officer's field cap. Although this service cap

A group of panzermen pose in front of their tanks in mid-1943, all wearing their black distinctive panzer uniforms, the black M1938 field cap and the later version black M1943 field cap. This latter featured flaps at the side that buttoned at the front of the cap. These flaps could be folded down and worn to protect the wearer's ears and to the side of the head. Although these later version caps were popular, this cap featured a peak that prevented easy access of the visor sights inside the tank, so the cap was sometimes seen being worn back to front.

was not technically an item designed for the panzer arm, it was still nonetheless an integral part of the panzer officer's uniform and was worn throughout the war.

The panzer uniform remained a well-liked and very popular item of clothing and did not alter materially during the war. However, in 1942 a special two-piece reed-green denim suit was issued to panzer crews in areas of operations where the climate was considered warmer than normal theaters of combat. The suit was hard wearing, light, and easy to wash, and many crews were seen wearing the uniform during the summer months. The uniform was generally worn by armored crews, maintenance personnel, and even panzergrenadiers operating with half-tracked vehicles, notably the Sd.Kfz.251 series. This popular and practical garment was identical in cut to the black panzer uniform. It consisted of the normal insignia, including the national emblem, panzer death's head collar patches and shoulder straps.

Apart from the uniforms worn by the panzer arm, crews of armored antitank units also initially wore the black panzer uniform. However, with the increased need on the battlefield for self-propelled assault gun and tank destroyer units in close support of infantry, it was considered that the black panzer uniform was unsuitable as crews were more exposed on the battlefield when they left their armored vehicles. Consequently, a special uniform was introduced for both *sturmartillerie* and *panzerjäger* units. The uniform was specially designed primarily to be worn inside and away from their armored vehicles, and for this reason designers produced a garment that offered better camouflage qualities than the standard black panzer uniform. The uniform worn by units of the *panzerjäger* was made entirely

Two tank men pose in front of their Tiger I in 1943. These men belong to the famous *schwere Panzer Abteilung 505*, the 505th Heavy Tank Battalion, which saw extensive action at Kursk. The panzerman standing on the left is the tank commander; his crewman next to him has just been decorated. They both wear the familiar black panzer uniform which was specially designed to allow the wearer plenty of movement inside the cramped confines of an armored vehicle. With no external pockets, this also minimized any material snagging on protruding parts of the tank.

A *sturmartillerie* enlisted man wears the special field-gray uniform of tank destroyer and self-propelled assault gun units. The style of the uniform was very similar to that of the black panzer uniform, but this garment was made entirely of field-gray cloth. The collar patches too differed from other units entitled to wear the uniform. The garment was a very practical piece of clothing, and, unlike the black panzer uniform, it was less conspicuous when the crewman left his vehicle.

from lightweight gray-green woolen material. The cut was very similar to that of the black panzer uniform. However, it did differ in respect of insignia and the collar patches.

The *panzerjäger* uniform was a very practical garment and it was identical to the cut of the *sturmartillerie* uniform, but with the exception of the color. The uniform was made entirely of field-gray cloth, but again differed in respect to certain insignia. The collar patches consisted of the death's head emblems, which were stitched on patches of dark blue-green cloth and were edged with bright red *Waffenfarbe* piping. However, officers did not display the death's head collar patches, but wore the field service collar patches instead. No piping on the collar patches was used either.

Like the summer two-piece reed-green panzer denim suit worn by panzer crews, both tank destroyer and self-propelled assault gun units also had their own working and summer uniforms, which were also produced in the same color and material.

Joseph Stalin. After the shock of *Barbarossa*, the Soviet supremo gradually transformed to become an arch-strategist, assisted by some sublime generals.

The Soviet Soldier in 1943

Since 1941 the Red Army had adapted their tactics against the superior fighting quality of the Germans. The Russians knew very well the greatest blunder committed by the German Supreme Command was underestimating the Soviets' capacity of putting vast numbers of men and weaponry into the field. They also knew that much of their fighting ability would depend on the vastness of Russia itself, their main ally. The sheer size of the battlefield and of the numbers which fought on it consequently overstretched their enemy, often to breaking point.

But it was not just the size of Russia and its climate that was a determining factor in the Red Army's gradual success: it was the leadership and the soldier himself. An infantryman's character in the Soviet army had undergone little change since the Crimean War. His upbringing too had taught him to be hard, resilient, determined, resourceful, and to be brave and bold in the face of adversity. As a soldier he adopted that same attitude when the Germans invaded his homeland. He had been driven back by well-trained and better-equipped soldiers, but fortunately for the Russian soldier, the enemy soon overreached himself, and with the advent of the winter his advance disastrously ground to a halt. This gave the Red Army time to re-equip and build defensive positions. Although the Germans were able to recover from the first winter, their forces were unable to resume an offensive along the entire front. Instead, only parts of the front resumed operations with the Soviets containing them wherever they could.

By the time it was conceived that the Wehrmacht was preparing a massive offensive in the Kursk region, the Red Army had already evolved into a massive defensive force with thousands of tanks and an ever-increasing array of supporting arms. Yet, the groundswell change in the Red Army was far beyond its huge arsenal. The tactics employed were primarily due to the conventional infantryman himself. Out in the field the soldier had adapted—often on the barrel of the political commissar—in a way that made him resilient and almost fanatical in the fight to the death for the Motherland.

The Soviet Soldier's Personal Equipment and Weapons

Compared to Germans, the Russians were fundamentally inferior in weaponry. However, infantry equipment, artillery, and tank design were simple, robust, conventional, effective, and often impressive.

A standard infantryman's personal equipment did not fundamentally change between 1941 and 1943. There existed two types of tunics and breeches worn by the soldier in 1943, the M35 and M43 patterns. Both were typically worn during Kursk. The side cap, or *pilotka*, was the standard headgear for the Red Army. Under battle conditions the M40 helmet, or *shlem*, was worn and did not change throughout the war.

Personal equipment comprised of one or two ammunition pouches for the Mosin Nagant rifle. For submachine guns, there were cloth pouches holding the drum magazines or long-style magazines. For the SVT-40 special leather pouches were used for holding the two magazines. Among other gear worn were the canteen, gasmask bag, rain cape (*plasch palatka*), backpack (*myeshok*), entrenching tool, greatcoat and/or the *telogreika* padded jacket.

The standard infantryman's weapon was the M91/30 Mosin Nagant bolt action rifle. The M38 Mosin Nagant carbine was also typically used, along with the SVT-40 Tokarev rifle. The PPSh-41 and PPSh-43 submachine guns were also used extensively and effectively on the battlefield.

Along the defensive lines at Kursk the Red Army typically armed their units with a vast array of weaponry, including the Maxim MP1910 machine gun, DP1928 light machine gun, 7.62mm SG1943 belt-fed machine gun, and PTRS and PTRD 1941 antitank rifles. Also issued were the 50mm mortar M1938–M1940, and 82mm mortar 1941-M1943. Larger calibers were also found including the 107mm, 120mm, and 160mm, which were issued to artillery units.

Supporting the infantry were the artillery and antitank gun regiments. These comprised the 37mm M1930, 45mm M1942 and 57mm antitank guns. The 76mm M1943 infantry gun was extensively employed along the front as were the 122mm howitzer M1938, and 152mm howitzer M1943.

The backbone of artillery support was the impressive Katyusha multiple rocket launcher. By the end of 1942, some 57 regiments were in service together with smaller independent battalions, all in all the equivalent of 216 batteries.

Soviet Preparations for Battle

For many months the Red Army had been preparing their defenses in the Kursk region, having preempted the German offensive in the area. Soviet intelligence had been receiving vast amounts of information about German troop concentrations in the Orel and Kharkov region, as well as decrypts from Bletchley Park in England and the Lucy spy ring in Switzerland, relating to an intended German offensive in the Kursk sector.

Whilst Hitler was planning his *Zitadelle* offensive, the Red Army was preparing its defense, unbeknown to German intelligence. Joseph Stalin had already increased war production in early 1943 to a level that the German industrial war machine could not match. Some 2,000 tanks and self-propelled guns and 2,500 aircraft were being mass-produced each month. In the Kursk salient alone there had been a massive buildup of Soviet forces in the first half of 1943. In April Marshal Georgi Zhukov had obtained improved intelligence from extensive Russian reconnaissance sorties, reports from Lucy (the codename for the Swiss-based Soviet agent), and from transmissions from British intelligence at Bletchley Park, to predict exactly the strategic focal point of where the German attack in the salient would be unleashed.

In a number of military conferences held during the

In a trench the soldier on the right is armed with an PTRS antitank rifle in an antiaircraft role. Whilst these rifles were used throughout the war, its armor-penetrating capabilities were limited. However, due to the limited amounts of antitank weapons available, it was a stop gap solution. Right of the antitank gunner is a soldier armed with a PPSh-41 submachine gun.

Lightly equipped Red Army soldiers move along a typical Soviet trench just prior to the offensive. They are armed with PPSh-41 submachine guns. This weapon, used extensively on the Eastern Front, was a magazine-fed, selective fire submachine gun using an open bolt, blowback action. It was made mainly of stamped steel, and could be fired either with a box or drum magazine. It was one of the major infantry weapons used by the Red Army with around six million of them manufactured.

An interesting photograph showing Russian sappers with a collection of German Teller mines laid out in front of a defensive position. The Teller mine was well designed, robust and reliable. However, due to their design features, the Russians were able to dig them up with comparative ease and reuse them against the Germans.

A cavalry unit of the Red Army on the march towards the front. Animal draught, even in 1943, was common in the Soviet army in spite of the growing might of their armored divisions.

An artillery crew moving a 76mm divisional gun M1942 (ZiS-3) into position along a treeline. Soviet gunners liked the ZiS-3 for its extreme reliability, durability, and accuracy. The gun was easy to maintain and could be operated by inexperienced crews. The light carriage allowed the ZiS-3 to be towed by trucks quickly and effectively, or even hauled by the crew. The gun had excellent anti-armor capabilities. Its armor-piercing round could disable German light and medium tanks, but not heavier armor such as the Tiger and the Panther.

spring Zhukov showed Stalin extensive intelligence reports outlining the movements of the Wehrmacht, and quickly identified that the enemy was preparing an attack in the Kursk salient. In a conference held on April 12, in front of Stalin, Zhukov concluded that in his opinion the Red Army should not preempt the enemy offensive, but to dig in and wait for him, wearing his forces down in a drawn-out, protracted defensive action. He concluded, much to the agreement of Stalin and other front line commanders, that the German offensive should be met and deliberately ground down in a defensive battle of attrition. Their main intention was to destroy the cream of the German armor and then incapacitate the enemy ground troops who would be exposed without armored support. Stalin agreed that his commanders should transform the Kursk salient into an impregnable fortress.

Whilst Hitler's arsenal gathered strength for the Kursk offensive, the Red Army prepared the largest concentration of strength ever seen on the Eastern Front. For every mile of defensive line there were some 4,500 soldiers, 45 tanks and 105 guns and mortars dug in. Around Voronezh, known to the Soviets as the Voronezh Front, about 2,500 men, 42 tanks and 59 guns and mortars were fielded in every mile of the sector. In total there were some 573,000 soldiers, 8,500 guns, mortars, and 1,600 tanks and self-propelled guns. Both the Central and Voronezh Fronts alone contained more than 1.3 million men, 20,000 artillery pieces and mortars, 3,500 tanks and self-propelled guns, and were supported in the air by some 2,600 aircraft.

Behind these defenses stood additional troops of the Steppe Front. Although only 295,000 of the Steppe Front reserve troops, including 900 tanks, would be moved forward during the battle, they had additional resources to commit another 20,000 men and 600 tanks should they be required. The total number of men available at Kursk was some 1,910,000 plus 5,000 tanks. These numbers dominated their German foe by about 2.5 to 1 in troops, and massively exceeded the Germans in both guns and tanks.

In a defensive positions Soviet troops armed with PPSh-41 submachine guns and antitank rifles are supported by a 76.2mm field gun concealed next to a tree. This weapon fired a 6.4kg shell and had a maximum range of 14,534 yards and, like most Soviet guns, an antitank capability with solid shot.

In Profile:
T-34-76 M43

The T-34 was a Soviet medium tank which came into production in its thousands in 1940. It possessed a good combination of firepower, mobility, protection, and ruggedness. Some 80,000 T-34s of all variants would be produced during World War II, and despite their massive losses in combat, their significant numbers meant they were still able to prove successful at Kursk, and for the remainder of the war. This vehicle is painted in olive green RAL 6003 with a tactical number 103 painted in yellow on the turret side. (Tom Cooper)

The vast majority of T-34s were fitted with an F-34 76.2mm gun. Their high-explosive rounds were able to penetrate any early German tank's armor at normal combat ranges. Against later uparmored panzers such as the Panther and Tiger, closer ranges were required, which then put tank crews at higher risk. Massive losses were inevitable. This example of a T-34 has a camouflage scheme of olive green RAL 6003. (Tom Cooper)

Sappers out along the front line in a minefield. The soldier nearest the camera is armed with a PPSh-41 submachine gun, whilst his comrade appears to be armed with an antitank rifle. Note the "hedgehog" antitank obstacles constructed from steel girders and often secured with concrete. Hedgehogs were designed to wreck the tracks and running gear of a tank if it became impaled on them.

A Soviet antitank gun crew moving towards the front. The commander raises his arm to signify a halt. Interestingly the antitank gun is a captured German PaK 35/36 antitank gun. Though this weapon was inadequate against heavier German armor, Russian antitank crews still found that the PaK was more than sufficient for operational needs in the face of relatively modest armored opposition such as support, reconnaissance, and halftrack vehicles.

Preparing for Attack

The Soviets had comprehensively prepared their defenses in special defensive zones and belts, littered with strongpoints and antitank obstacles. The defenses comprised more than six major defensive belts, each of which was subdivided into two or even three layers of almost impregnable strongholds. The first two belts were manned by frontline troops, while the third and fourth consisted of reserve units. The last two belts were virtually empty of troops, and used mainly to drip-feed reserves into the defensive belts as cannon fodder. It was planned that if the Germans were to ever break through all the defensive belts, they would still have to confront a number of additional belts constructed east of the Kursk salient under the direction of General Ivan Konev's Steppe Military District, shortly renamed the Steppe Front.

However, the Red Army deduced that the Germans would never reach these additional belts, as each belt was some 200 to 250 miles deep. Each comprised hundreds of strongpoints and extensive networks of obstacles. Spread among these belts were well-armed troops with antitank rifles and machine-gun positions dug in amongst a maze of intricate blockhouses and trenches. Towns and villages that fell in the path of these belts were evacuated. More than 350,000 women, children and old men were removed from their homes and press-ganged into service to help construct antitank ditches and other obstacles.

In the Voronezh Front, for instance, there were some 420 miles of antitank obstacles and more than 3,700 miles of trenches. In addition there were thousands of antipersonnel and antitank mines installed with additional artillery shells buried in the ground and detonated remotely.

Troops move forward to support a defensive line. The soldiers are wearing the basic kit of a Soviet soldier, including the blanket with haversack, gasmask cape and rolled ground sheet. Note the machine-gun crew pulling the 1910 Maxim machine gun. To the right is a mortar crew armed with the 50mm M1940 mortar.

A typical strongpoint comprised an antitank rifle company or battalion, a sapper platoon, an artillery company, and two or three tanks or self-propelled guns. T-34 tanks were buried at intervals up to their turrets, alongside self-propelled tank destroyers and artillery pieces.

The battle of Kursk was probably the first modern Soviet operation since the Germans had invaded the country in June 1941. Although the Red Army lacked the technological superiority of individual weaponry, with their sturdy T-34 tanks they were well prepared to deal with the enemy's new Tiger and Panther tanks and his elite forces of the Waffen-SS.

In addition to their defenses, the Red Army implemented preparations for elaborate deception plans in order to confuse the enemy. This consisted of concealing troop concentrations and defensive positions by constructing false trenches, dummy tanks and artillery, and even false airfields. All Red Army troop and rail movements were conducted at night or when visibility limited the enemy from conducting aerial reconnaissance missions.

Preparations for the imminent attack continued even when the Germans opened their massive artillery bombardment. Russian soldiers had been well trained in how to overcome the natural fear of an approaching Tiger tank or a similar deadly armored vehicle. They had been drilled on various defensive tactics that included counterattacking the enemy infantry following behind the tanks. Every soldier was given preplanned targets and killing zones. Although the average Russian soldier doubted his self-belief in resisting the Germans, his commanders—and the ubiquitous political commissars behind the troops—gave him the comfort that they were well prepared in their great labyrinth of defensive positions.

In early July 1943, as the Germans prepared to unleash their fury, Russian soldiers, after months of preparation were ready, sitting in their bunkers, trenches and other well dug-in positions for the first sign of an attack. The final showdown was about to begin.

An M1943 mortar crew sight their weapon. This heavy mortar, known as the Samova, was a 120mm smoothbore mortar first introduced in 1943 as a modified version of the M1938. It was muzzle-loaded and could easily be broken down into three parts: base plate, barrel, and bipod. The crew could then easily transport the mortar over short distances, often towed by a GAZ-66 vehicle or on a two-wheel tubular carriage.

In Profile:
Captain, Russian tanker, 5th Tank Guards

This Red Army officer wears a typical early tank overall complete with leather overcoat, and padded leather helmet. Black and red service colors are applied on both collars, complemented by vertical bars in red (indicating the rank of a captain), and a metallic badge representing a tank. Thick leather gloves and knee boots are worn with the uniform. This was relatively heavy clothing, usually replaced by simple overalls of blue fabric in the summer. However, due to shortage in supplies, this type of early overall was still seen in the ranks of the Red Army in 1943. (Tom Cooper)

Red Army Order of Battle, Kursk 1943

WESTERN FRONT (V. Sokolovsky)

50th Army (I. Boldin)

38th Rifle Corps
17th Rifle Division
326th Rifle Division
413th Rifle Division
49th Rifle Division
64th Rifle Division
212th Rifle Division
324th Rifle Division

11th Guards Army (I. Bagramjan)

8th Guards Rifle Corps
11th Guards Rifle Division
26th Guards Rifle Division
83rd Guards Rifle Division
16th Guards Rifle Corps
1st Guards Rifle Division
16th Guards Rifle Division
31st Guards Rifle Division
169th Rifle Division
36th Guards Rifle Corps
5th Guards Rifle Division
18th Guards Rifle Division
84st Guards Rifle Division
108th Rifle Division
217th Rifle Division

1st Air Army (M. Gromov)

2nd Assault Air Corps
2nd Fighter Air Corps
8th Fighter Air Corps

Front assets

1st Independent Tank Corps
5th Independent Tank Corps

BRYANSK FRONT (M. Popov)

3rd Army (A. Gorbatov)

41st Rifle Corps
235th Rifle Division
308th Rifle Division
380th Rifle Division
269th Rifle Division
283rd Rifle Division
342nd Rifle Division

61st Army (P. Belov)

9th Guards Rifle Corps
12th Guards Rifle Division
76th Guards Rifle Division
77th Guards Rifle Division
97th Rifle Division
110th Rifle Division
336th Rifle Division
356th Rifle Division
415th Rifle Division

63rd Army (V. Kolpakty)

5th Rifle Division
41st Rifle Division
129th Rifle Division
250th Rifle Division
287th Rifle Division
348th Rifle Division
397th Rifle Division

15th Air Army (N. Naumenko)

1st Guards Fighter Air Corps
1st Independent Guards Tank Corps
3rd Assault Air Corps
25th Rifle Corps
186th Rifle Division
283rd Rifle Division
362nd Rifle Division

CENTRAL FRONT (Konstantin Rokossovsky)

13th Army (N. Puchov)

17th Guards Rifle Corps
6th Guards Rifle Division
70th Guards Rifle Division
75th Guards Rifle Division
18th Guards Rifle Corps
2nd Airborne Guards Rifle Division
3rd Airborne Guards Rifle Division
4th Airborne Guards Rifle Division
15th Rifle Corps
8th Rifle Division
74th Rifle Division
148th Rifle Division
29th Rifle Corps
15th Rifle Division
81st Rifle Division
307th Rifle Division

48th Army (P. Romanenko)

42nd Rifle Corps
16th Rifle Division
202nd Rifle Division
399th Rifle Division
73rd Rifle Division
137th Rifle Division
143rd Rifle Division
170th Rifle Division

60th Army (I. Chernyakhovsky)

24th Rifle Corps
42nd Rifle Division
112th Rifle Division
30th Rifle Corps
121st Rifle Division
141st Rifle Division
322nd Rifle Division
Independent 55th Rifle Division

65th Army (P. Batov)

18th Rifle Corps
69th Rifle Division
149th Rifle Division
246th Rifle Division
27th Rifle Corps
60th Rifle Division
193rd Rifle Division
37th Guards Rifle Division
181st Rifle Division
194th Rifle Division
354th Rifle Division

70th Army (I. Galanin)

28th Rifle Corps
132nd Rifle Division
211th Rifle Division
280th Rifle Division
102nd Rifle Division
106th Rifle Division
140th Rifle Division
162nd Rifle Division
354th Rifle Division

2nd Tank Army (A. Rodin)

3rd Tank Corps
16th Tank Corps

16th Air Army (S. Rudenko)

3rd Bombing Air Corps
6th Mixed Air Corps
6th Fighter Air Corps
Independent 9th Tank Corps
Independent 19th Tank Corps

VORONEZH FRONT (N. VATUTIN)

6th Guards Army (I. Chistiakov)

22nd Guards Rifle Corps
67th Guards Rifle Division
71st Guards Rifle Division
90th Guards Rifle Division
23rd Guards Rifle Corps
51st Guards Rifle Division
52nd Guards Rifle Division
375th Rifle Division
Independent 89th Guards Rifle Division

7th Guards Army (M. Shumilov)

24th Guards Rifle Corps
15th Guards Rifle Division
36st Guards Rifle Division
72nd Guards Rifle Division
25th Guards Rifle Corps
73rd Guards Rifle Division
78th Guards Rifle Division
81st Guards Rifle Division
Independent 213th Rifle Division

38th Army (N. Chibisov)

50th Rifle Corps
167th Rifle Division
232nd Rifle Division
340th Rifle Division
51st Rifle Corps
180th Rifle Division
240th Rifle Division
Independent 204th Rifle Division

40th Army (K. Moskalenko)

47th Rifle Corps
161st Rifle Division
206th Rifle Division
237th Rifle Division
52nd Rifle Corps
100th Rifle Division
219th Rifle Division
309th Rifle Division
Independent 184th Rifle Division

69th Army (V. Kruchenkin)

48th Rifle Corps
107th Rifle Division
183rd Rifle Division
307th Rifle Division
49th Rifle Corps
111th Rifle Division
270th Rifle Division

1st Tank Army (M. Katukov)

6th Tank Corps
31st Tank Corps
3rd Mechanized Corps

2nd Air Army (S. Krasovskii)

1st Bombing Air Corps
1st Assault Air Corps
4th Fighter Air Corps
5th Fighter Air Corps
35th Guards Rifle Corps
92nd Guards Rifle Division
93rd Guards Rifle Division
94th Guards Rifle Division
Independent 2nd Guards Tank Corps
Independent 3rd Guards Tank Corps

STEPPE FRONT (Ivan Konev)

5th Guards Army (A. Zhadov)

32nd Guards Rifle Corps
13th Guards Rifle Division
66th Guards Rifle Division
6th Airborne Guards Rifle Division
33rd Guards Rifle Corps
95th Guards Rifle Division
97th Guards Rifle Division
9th Airborne Guards Rifle Division
Independent 42nd Guards Rifle Division
Independent 10th Tank Corps

5th Guards Tank Army (Pavel Rotmistrov)

5th Guards Mechanized Corps
29th Tank Corps

5th Air Army (S. Gorunov)

7th Mixed Air Corps
8th Mixed Air Corps
3rd Fighter Air Corps
7th Fighter Air Corps

An interesting photograph showing a battery of Hummel panzerjägers loaded onto a special railway flatcar. Some 100 Hummels participated in the Kursk offensive and were successful in a number of engagements. They served in the armored artillery battalions, or *panzerartillerie abteilungen*, of the Panzer divisions, forming separate heavy self-propelled artillery batteries, each with six Hummels and one ammunition carrier.

German Preparations for Battle

By June 1943, German plans for the Kursk offensive, codenamed Operation *Zitadelle*, were finally issued to all the commanders in the field. The plan was for the Wehrmacht to smash Red Army formations and leave the road to Moscow open. For this daring offensive, the German forces were distributed between Army Group Center and Army Group South.

Whilst the Red Army were preparing defensive positions, the Germans were getting ready for a massive offensive against the Kursk salient. For some months the Germans had amassed over 780,000 men, almost 10,000 guns and mortars, 2,900 tanks and assault guns, and some 2,500 aircraft.

A Pz.Kpfw.V Panther tank on a special railway flatcar being readied for the front. In June 1943, 21 panzer divisions, including four Waffen-SS divisions and two panzergrenadier divisions, were preparing for Operation *Zitadelle* in the Kursk salient.

For the first time in many months, in March 1943, Adolf Hitler began displaying a growing appetite for a large-scale offensive on the Eastern Front, and at his mountain retreat at the Berghof he began deliberating such an operation. The new offensive that he had been planning was a big gamble. But he was still confident that he could repeat earlier, devastating victories against the Soviets.

At a number of conferences held in the early spring Hitler began openly discussing a very tempting strategy opportunity that he optimistically believed would bring his Panzerwaffe victory. The key was the city of Kursk, positioned 150 miles north of Kharkov

Another photograph showing the transportation of a Pz.Kpfw.V Panther tank to the front by train. For the offensive the Panzerwaffe were able to muster in early July 17 divisions and two brigades with no fewer than 1,715 panzers and 147 Sturmegeschutz III (StuG) assault guns. Each division averaged some 98 panzers and self-propelled antitank guns. The Panther Ausf.A made its debut, despite its production problems.

Kurt Zeitzler

Kurt Zeitzler was a Chief of the Army General Staff in the Wehrmacht who was known for his energy, determination and forthright opinions in front of Hitler. Because of his ability in managing the movement of large mobile formations, it was Zeitzler who planned the troop movements and general outline for Operation *Zitadelle*.

at an important railway junction in the center of a vast salient, measuring some 120 miles wide and 75 miles deep. Hitler asked his generals whether they could muster enough armor and infantry to attack from the north and south of the salient in a huge pincer movement and encircle the Red Army dug in along defensive positions around Kursk. In Hitler's view, the offensive would be the greatest armored battle ever conducted on the Eastern Front and that would include the bulk of his mighty Panzerwaffe, among them premier Waffen-SS divisions, the cream of his fighting force.

On April 21, General Kurt Zeitzler, Hitler's Chief of Staff, made a special flight to Berchtesgaden in order to try and convince the Führer not to abandon the offensive, drafted as "Order 6." A few days later General Model, commander of the Ninth Army, arrived at the Berghof. In a two-hour meeting he presented Hitler with aerial photographs proving that the Soviets were building strong defensive lines, some of which were impregnable. Hitler decided to cancel the offensive until May 5.

A specially adapted flatbed train loaded with Tiger tanks preparing to be transported to the front. The main factor in the success of the panzer divisions on the Eastern Front was their ability to swiftly reach threatened sectors of the front.

A Tiger I belonging to *schwere Panzer Abteilung 503* during field exercises in 1943. The battalion saw extensive combat in Army Group Don in early 1943 and served with a number of divisions of the Fourth Panzer Army, where it was tasked with securing the withdrawal of Army Group A. The unit took part in March 1943 in the Third Battle for Kharkov and then received a full complement of 45 Tigers in May in preparation for the Kursk offensive.

A Pz.Kpfw.III command vehicle fords a river during the initial stages of the Kursk offensive.

Panther tanks and other equipment have been loaded on special railway flatbeds destined for the front line on the Eastern Front. The Panther tank was rushed out of the factory so that it could participate in the Kursk offensive.

On April 29, Hitler again postponed the attack until the 9th, in order to allow more time for additional reinforcements to be brought to the front, including the new Panther tank. When his panzer expert, General Heinz Guderian, arrived at the Berghof a few days later he inquired why the Führer wanted to start another offensive at all in the East in 1943. Hitler replied that he had doubts himself, and it made him feel very anxious thinking about it, but he could not let a whole year pass by on the defensive. Guderian said that he needed more time to furnish the front with additional armor before *Zitadelle* could be unleashed and that a postponement of at least six weeks should allow sufficient time. Hitler agreed and throughout June the final plans for *Zitadelle* were

An impressive number of StuG.III assault guns on the way to the front. In spite of the numerous advantages of the assault guns, equipping the panzer units with these vehicles did not meld well with the nature of the panzer. Yet, because of the lack of tanks in the dwindling ranks of the panzer divisions, the StuG.III was used alongside the panzer during the Kursk offensive, and proved very successful.

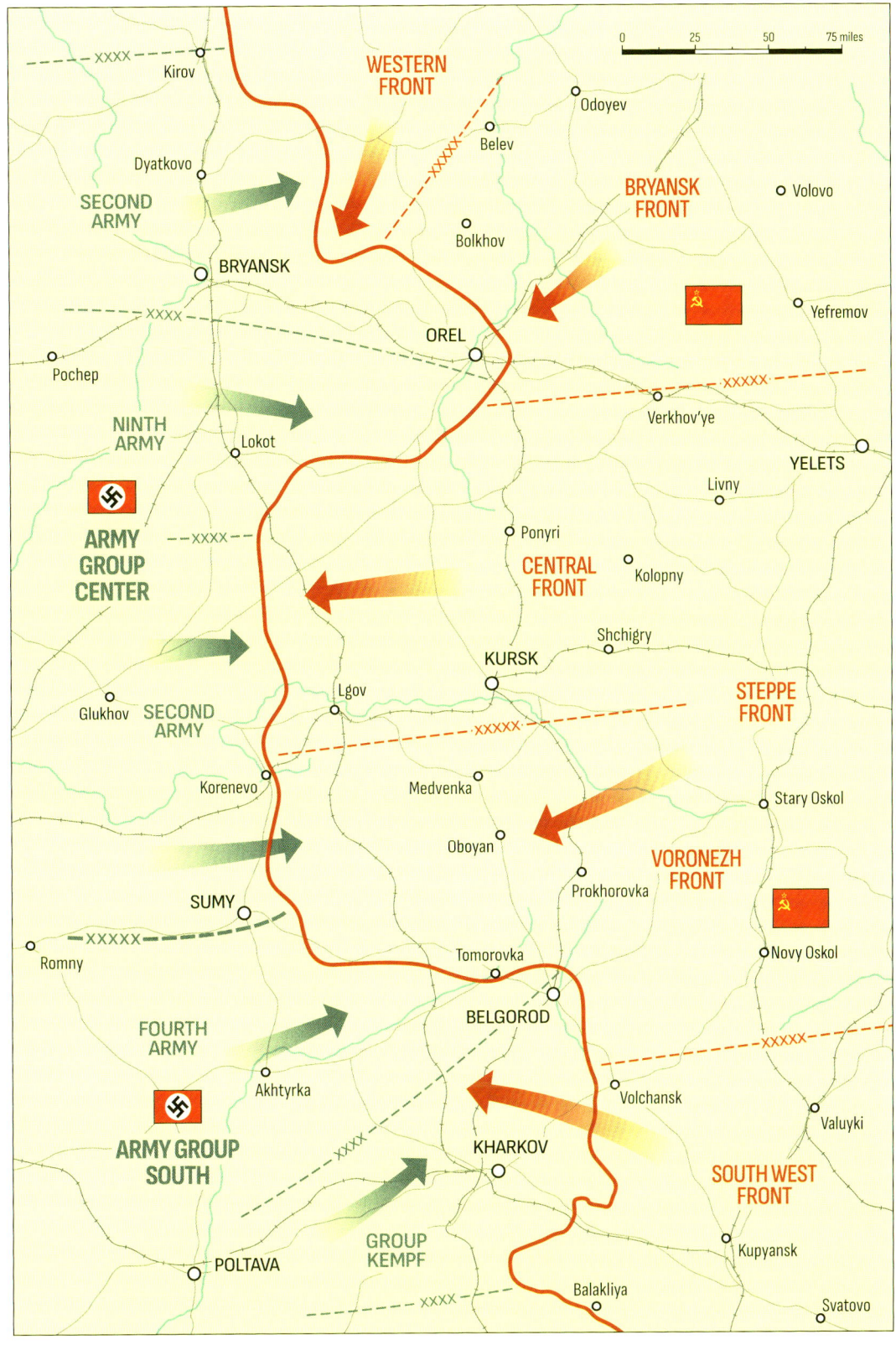

The German front line and the planned drive of Army Groups Center and North against the Red Army Western, Bryansk, Central, Steppe, and Voronezh Fronts on July 5, 1943.

A Panther Ausf.D variant moving across a field prior to the attack in late June or early July 1943.

systematically drawn up. In order to keep the offensive secret Hitler instructed OKW—Oberkommando der Wehrmacht, the High Command of the Armed Forces—not to publicize the plans.

A column of support vehicles moving to the front prior to the Kursk offensive. Note how the vehicles have turned the road into a quagmire.

The crew of a Pz.Kpfw. IV prepare their vehicle for the Kursk operation. Note the track links bolted to the front plates of the tank for additional armored protection.

The crew of a Marder III tank destroyer pose in front of their machine. The Marder was the first of a series of improvised light tank hunters, and was built on the chassis of a Pz.Kpfw.38 (t). This particular vehicle is fitted with a captured 7.62cm Russian 36 antitank gun.

German Preparations for Battle

The crew of a Marder III with their tank destroyer in preparation for the offensive. Whilst the vehicle was relatively successful at Kursk, it offered the crew little protection.

A Tiger tank in the lee of a building being prepared by its crew. Note that the tank's muzzle break and machine guns have be "tarped" for protection against dirt and dust, a clear indication that this vehicle is not yet battle-ready.

Whilst Hitler received reports of the final troop movements for *Zitadelle*, on July 1, after spending almost six weeks at the Berghof, the Führer and staff transferred back to East Prussia. That same evening Hitler addressed his commanders gathered at Zeitzler's headquarters. In a clear, confident voice he explained the importance of the offensive, but made it known that the operation had limited objectives. He concluded that he did not want his forces becoming immersed, as they had done at Stalingrad, in a long, drawn-out contest of bitter attrition. He knew the offensive was a big gamble, and if it failed the consequences could be militarily devastating for German operations on the Eastern Front.

By June, plans for *Zitadelle* were issued to all the commanders in the field, in which it was proposed, quite simply, that the Wehrmacht was to attack and overrun Red Army formations and defenses, and force the road to Moscow.

Deployed in the center was General Walter Model's Ninth Army consisting of 21 German and three Hungarian divisions with over 335,000 men. The Hungarian divisions were tasked primarily with reconnaissance duties, mine-clearance, anti-partisan operations and security. Among the 21 German divisions, there were three panzer divisions, all distributed among XLVII, XLVI, XLI, XX, and XXIII Corps. The armored divisions of XLVII Corps were equipped with Pz.Kpfw.IIIs, and IVs, and StuG.IIIs, but the 21st Brigade boasted three Tiger tank companies in the 505th Heavy Tank Battalion with 45 Tigers and 15 Pz.Kpfw.IIIs.

XLI Corps comprised the heavy tank destroyer detachments recently refurbished with the entire production run of the Tiger panzerjägers, the "Ferdinands," as well as 66 Sturmpanzer IVs, nicknamed the "Grizzly Bear."

At a command post an Sd.Kfz.251 halftrack can be seen parked next to a support vehicle. Some of the crewmembers are conversing near a tent.

Waiting for the offensive. Two crewmembers of an Sd.Kfz.251 can be seen resting on the engine deck of their vehicle. Note how all the vehicles are purposely spread out across the steppe in order to present a smaller target in case of ground or aerial bombardment.

The crew of a well-concealed Sd.Kz.251 halftrack relax next to their vehicle.

An Sd.Kfz.251 crew pose in front of their halftrack during preparations for the Kursk offensive.

An infantryman standing next to a 15cm howitzer on tow. As the standard heavy field howitzer in the Wehrmacht, the gun was very effective at breaching heavily concentrated positions to let tanks and infantry pour through unhindered. It would be these guns that would open the bombardment during the opening phase of Kursk.

An artillery observation post. A gunner is peering through a tripod-mounted 6x30 Sf.14Z *scherenfernrohr* (scissor binoculars). Each artillery battery had an observation post among the frontline positions.

A 15cm sFH 18 being prepared for a fire mission. This weapon was the standard piece in a German division. Employment of artillery was a necessity to any ground force engaging the enemy.

Two photographs taken in sequence showing a well-camouflaged 15cm howitzer out in the field being prepared for a fire mission. Three of the gunners are shirtless, which is a clear indication of the high daytime temperatures and the amount of exertion required to get the gun battle-ready.

Two 15cm howitzer crewmembers sit on the gun trails. This gun was the workhorse of the German artillery, providing the division with a relatively effective mobile fire base. The artillery regiments were primarily given the task of destroying enemy positions and fortified defenses and conducting counterbattery fire prior to an armored assault.

A Luftwaffe flak crew in the field with their 8.8cm FlaK gun. This flak gun was used in two roles: as a mobile heavy antiaircraft piece, and also in a more static role for defense against aerial attack. The gun is bolted on a cruciform platform from which it fired with outriggers extended. At Kursk the Germans had already recognized that the heavier and more lethal Soviet armor was stacking up against the Wehrmacht and for this reason German forces clamored to obtain more flak guns that could deal with the increasing threat.

An 8.8cm flak gun in a static position. With Soviet aircraft increasing their dominance in the skies, the German divisions were compelled to further increase the size of their antiaircraft battalions, with each containing two or even three heavy batteries. This flak gun, complete with *schützschild* (splinter shield), shows off the kill ring markings on its barrel.

In the south was General Hermann Hoth's Fourth Panzer Army, with over 350,000 soldiers supported by Tiger tanks and the new Panther tanks. Army Group South was equipped with the largest contingent of armored vehicles, infantry and artillery, far larger than the Ninth Army of Army Group Center. Whilst Ninth Army comprised some 988 tanks and assault guns, the Fourth Panzer Army and Army Detachment Kempf boasted some 1,377 tanks and assault guns.

Army Group South consisted of III, XI, XLII, and XXIV Panzer Corps. The III Panzer Corps consisted of 299 tanks and 25 StuG.IIIs including the 503rd Panzer Detachment with 45 Tigers. XI Corps had 25 StuG.IIIs distributed between the 905th and 393rd Assault Gun Detachments. XLII Corps numbered 40 tank destroyers comprising the Nashorn and a heavy tank destroyer detachment of 40 assault guns. XXIV Panzer Corps included the 17th Panzer Division and was supported by the elite force of the 5th SS Panzer Division Wiking, equipped with 112 tanks.

Prior to the Kursk offensive some 2,816 panzers and self-propelled assault guns were manufactured. Of these 156 were Tigers, and 48 Panthers. For Kursk alone 211 Tigers, 259 Panthers, and 90 Ferdinands were brought to the front. The Panthers were distributed between two new Panther battalions, the 51st and 52nd Panther Battalions. These arrived on June 30 and July 1 and were attached to the Grossdeutschland Division in the XLVIII Panzer Corps of Army Group South. This panzer corps was commanded by General Schmidt von Knobelsdorff and comprised the 3rd and 11th Panzer Divisions and the 167th Infantry Division.

A flak crew rest next to their 2cm flak gun. Once the gun was leveled by three adjustable feet, the gun layer would then climb into the seat and the gun would be ready for action. Note in the distance a radio vehicle fitted with long-range antennae.

This 15cm howitzer concealed under camouflage netting is in an elevated position being prepared for action. These heavy field guns could hurl a destructive charge miles into the enemy lines, with devastating results.

Although the German arsenal looked impressive on paper, massive losses the previous winter had resulted in radical reductions in troop strengths. As a consequence, there was greater than normal variation in divisional size and strength. In theory a typical panzer division in 1943 had an average strength of around 175–200 armored vehicles and 15,500 men, organized into a tank regiment of two or even three battalions, an artillery regiment, a panzergrenadier brigade, and divisional support units. At Kursk the Germans could only muster around 70 armored vehicles per division, the strongest of which were the three Waffen-SS panzergrenadier divisions of II SS Panzer Corps, and the Heer panzergrenadier division Grossdeutschland. The SS Leibstandarte Adolf Hitler, SS Das Reich and SS Totenkopf had the strongest contingent of armored vehicles, comprising on average 130 panzers and 35 assault guns with Grossdeutschland boasting some 160 panzers and 35 assault guns.

The commonest armored vehicles that were used for the offensive were the Pz.Kpfw. IIIs and IVs. These, together with the powerful Tiger and Panther tanks, which were still an unknown quantity at this time, were given the daunting task of smashing through the Soviet defensive belts. Because troop strengths within the panzer and infantry divisions were lower than normal, huge pressure was placed upon the Panzerwaffe to achieve greater results by taking on more ambitious tasks usually reserved for the infantry.

Spread out across a field are a number of Sd.Kfz.251 halftracks. The Sd.Kfz.251 became the most popular halftrack used during the war and was utilized not only to carry troops into battle, but to tow ordnance and transport matériel.

The Panzer Divisions at Kursk, July 1943

2nd Panzer Division
Formed in October 1935 at Wurzburg

Divisional insignia

For the invasion of Russia the division used a new inverted "Y" with one mark. In mid-1943 a white trident symbol replaced this emblem, which was used for the remainder of the war.

Sub-units

2nd, 304th Panzergrenadier Regiments
3rd Panzer Regiment
74th Panzer Artillery Regiment
2nd Panzer Aufkl Abt (Reconnaissance)

Theaters of operation

Army Group Center (Smolensk, Orel, Kiev, Kursk) 1942–1943
France and Germany 1944–1945

3rd Panzer Division
Formed in October 1935 at Berlin

Divisional insignia

For the invasion of Russia a new symbol was introduced and regarded as the official symbol. It was an inverted yellow "Y" with two marks. However, units of the division could still use the bear in a white shield, and the tanks in the 6th Panzer Regiment also used the standing bear without a shield. The bear was often painted in various colors that included, white, yellow, blue, and red. In 1943 the 6th Panzer Regiment adopted a regimental emblem that was comprised of a black shield, round on the bottom and flat on top, with the 1939/40 divisional symbol of the 4th Panzer Division, and a pair of crossed swords below this.

Sub-units

3rd, 394th Panzergrenadier Regiments
6th Panzer Regiment
75th Panzer Artillery Regiment
3rd Panzer Aufkl Abt (Reconnaissance)

Theaters of operation

Central Russia 1941–1942
Kursk, Kharkov, Dnepr Bend 1943
Ukraine, Poland 1944
Hungary, Austria 1944–1945

4th Panzer Division
Formed in November 1938 at Wurzburg

Divisional insignia

In 1941 for the Russian campaign the division used the inverted "Y" with three marks, and used this for the remainder of the war.

Sub-units

12th, 33rd Panzergrenadier Regiments
35th Panzer Regiment
103rd Panzer Artillery Regiment
4th Panzer Aufkl Abt (Reconnaissance)

Theaters of operation

Central Russia (Caucasus 1942, Kursk 1943)
Latvia 1944
Germany 1945

5th Panzer Division
Formed in November 1939 at Oppeln

Divisional insignia

On the Eastern Front the 31st Panzer Regiment adopted the red devil's head as a regimental symbol. Together with the yellow "X" this was used until the end of the war.

Sub-units

13th, 14th Panzergrenadier Regiments
31st Panzer Regiment
116th Panzer Artillery Regiment
5th Panzer Aufkl Abt (Reconnaissance)

Theaters of operation

Central Russia (Kursk, Dnepr) 1941–1943
Latvia, Courland, East Prussia 1944–1945

6th Panzer Division
Formed in October 1939 at Wuppertal

Divisional insignia

For Kursk the symbol "X" in yellow was used.

Sub-units

4th, 114th Panzergrenadier Regiments
11th Panzer Regiment
76th Panzer Artillery Regiment
6th Panzer Aufkl Abt (Reconnaissance)

Theaters of operation

Russia 1941–1944
Hungary, Austria 1944–1945

7th Panzer Division
Formed in October 1939 at Weimar

Divisional insignia

For the Kursk operation armored vehicles used a yellow "Y" which was retained until the end of the war.

Sub-units

6th, 7th Panzergrenadier Regiments
25th Panzer Regiment
78th Panzer Artillery Regiment
7th Panzer Aufkl Abt (Reconnaissance)

Theaters of operation

Central Russia 1941
Refit in France 1942
Southern Russia 1942
Kharkov 1942
Kursk 1943
Baltic Coast, Prussia 1944–1945

8th Panzer Division
Formed in October 1938 at Berlin

Divisional insignia

In Russia the division used a new symbol, a yellow "Y" with one yellow mark, which was used until the end of the war.

Sub-units

8th, 28th Panzergrenadier Regiments
10th Panzer Regiment
80th Panzer Artillery Regiment
8th Panzer Aufkl Abt (Reconnaissance)

Theaters of operation

Southern Russia 1941
Central Russia 1942
Kursk 1943

11th Panzer Division
Formed in August 1940 at Breslau

Divisional insignia

This division was issued the official symbol of a yellow circle divided by a vertical bar. The division's unofficial emblem was a white-stenciled figure of a ghost brandishing a sword, which is why the division was known as the "Ghost" division.

Sub-units

110th, 111th Panzergrenadier Regiments
15th Panzer Regiment
119th Panzer Artillery Regimen
11th Panzer Aufkl Abt (Reconnaissance)

Theaters of operation

Russia (Orel, Belgorod, Krivoi Rog, Korsun) 1941–1944
Northern France 1944

12th Panzer Division
Formed in October 1940

Divisional insignia

The symbol was a yellow circle divided into three equal segments by "Y" which was retained until the end of the war.

Sub-units

5th, 25th Panzergrenadier Regiments
29th Panzer Regiment
2nd Panzer Artillery Regiment
12th Panzer Aufkl Abt (Reconnaissance)

Theaters of operation

Minsk, Smolensk 1941
Leningrad 1942
Orel, Middle Dnepr 1943
Courland 1945

17th Panzer Division
Formed in October 1940

Divisional insignia

This emblem was a yellow "Y" with two bars across the shaft.

Sub-units

40th, 63rd Panzergrenadier Regiments
39th Panzer Regiment 39
27th Panzer Artillery Regiment
17th Panzer Aufkl Abt (Reconnaissance)

Theaters of operation

Russia (Central and Southern Sectors) 1941–1943

18th Panzer Division
Formed in October 1940

Divisional insignia
The division's symbol was a yellow "Y" with three bars across its shaft. The 8th Panzer Brigade had a special marking, but this was not an official divisional emblem: a shield edged white, with a white skull and lines of water in white. The division was disbanded in 1943 and was reorganized as an artillery division, but continued using the same divisional symbol.

Sub-units
52nd, 101st Panzergrenadier Regiments
18th Panzer Regiment
88th Panzer Artillery Regiment 88
8th Panzer Aufkl Abt (Reconnaissance)

Theaters of operation
Russia (Central and Southern Sectors) 1941–1943

19th Panzer Division
Formed in October 1940

Divisional insignia
Because of the area where the division was formed, it adopted a yellow wolf-trap insignia.

Sub-units
73rd, 74th Panzergrenadier Regiments
27th Panzer Regiment
19th Panzer Artillery Regiment
19th Panzer Aufkl Abt (Reconnaissance)

Theaters of operation
Russia (Central and Southern Sectors) 1941–1943

20th Panzer Division
Formed in October 1940

Divisional insignia
Its symbol was a yellow "E" on its side, arms down, identical to the early 3rd Panzer Division emblem. In late 1943 the division received a new divisional insignia, which was a yellow arrow breaking through a curved borderline.

Sub-units
59th, 112th Panzergrenadier Regiments
21st Panzer Regiment
92nd Panzer Artillery Regiment
20th Panzer Aufkl Abt (Reconnaissance)

Theaters of operation
Moscow 1941
Orel 1943
Rumania 1944
East Prussia 1944
Hungary 1944

A battery of 15cm Nebelwerfer 41 launchers firing simultaneously during a fire mission. This weapon fired 2.5kg shells that could be projected over a range of 7,000 meters. When fired the projectiles screamed through the air, with the effect of unnerving the enemy. Because it was dangerous for the crew to be close to the launcher while the piece was being fired, it was done remotely using an electrical detonator attached to a cable.

Army Group Center

For the offensive the Germans committed two army groups, Army Group Center and Army Group South. In Army Group Center the Ninth Army was deployed on the northern side of the salient, consisting of 335,000 troops.

The Battle

For the offensive in Army Group Center, Model's main attack was to be undertaken by XLVII Panzer Corps, supported by 45 Tigers of the attached 505th Heavy Tank Battalion. Positioned on the left flank was XLI Panzer Corps, which comprised an attached regiment of 83 Ferdinand tank destroyers. On the right flank was XLVI Panzer Corps comprising four

Order of Battle, July 1943

ARMY GROUP CENTER (Günther von Kluge)

SECOND PANZER ARMY (Erich-Heinrich Cloessner)

XXXV Corps (Lothar Rendulic)

34th Infantry Division
56th Infantry Division
262nd Infantry Division
299th Infantry Division

LIII Corps (F. Gollwitzer)

208th Infantry Division
211th Infantry Division
293rd Infantry Division
25th Panzergrenadier Division

LV Corps (E. Jaschke)

110th Infantry Division
134th Infantry Division
296th Infantry Division
339th Infantry Division
Army Reserve
112th Infantry Division

SECOND ARMY (W. Weiss)

VII Corps (E.-E. Hell)

26th Infantry Division
68th Infantry Division
75th Infantry Division
88th Infantry Division

XIII Corps (E. Straube)

82nd Infantry Division
327th Infantry Division
340th Infantry Division

Army Group Reserve

5th Panzer Division
8th Panzer Division

NINTH ARMY (Walther Model)

XX Corps (R. von Roman)

45th Infantry Division
72nd Infantry Division
137th Infantry Division
251st Infantry Division

XLVI Panzer Corps (H. Zorn)

7th Infantry Division
31st Infantry Division
102nd Infantry Division
258th Infantry Division

XLI Panzer Corps (J. Harpe)

18th Panzer Division
86th Infantry Division
292nd Infantry Division

XLVII Panzer Corps (J. Lemelsen)

2nd Panzer Division
9th Panzer Division
20th Panzer Division
6th Infantry Division

XXIII Corps (J. Freissner)

216th Infantry Division
383rd Infantry Division
78th Assault Division

Army Reserve

4th Panzer Division
10th Panzergrenadier Division
12th Panzer Division

In Profile: Tanks and vehicles of *Zitadelle*

Pz.Kpfw.IV Ausf.H The Ausf.H version entered production in April 1943, and received the designation Sd. Kfz. 161/2. This variant saw the integrity of the glacis armor improved by manufacturing it as a single 80mm plate. For the first time antimine paste known as *zimmerit* was added to all the vertical services of the tank armor (though not on this particular variant). The vehicle's side and turret were further protected by the addition of 5mm side-skirts and 8mm turret-skirts. Various other modifications were made to this vehicle which included replacing the rubber return rollers with cast steel. The hull also was fitted with triangular supports for the easily damaged side-skirts. This tank has been upgraded with the new *schürzen* and painted in a sand base of dark yellow RAL 7028 with a camouflage scheme of large olive green RAL 6003 and brown RAL 8020 patches. (Tom Cooper)

Panther V Ausf.D Sd.Kfz. 171 This Panther from the 6th Kompanie Abteilung 52 39th Panzer-Regiment was fitted with two MG34s, one located co-axially with the main gun on the gun mantlet and an identical MG34 located on the glacis plate and fired by the radio operator. The Ausf.D and early Ausf.A variants used a "letterbox" flap enclosing its underlying thin, vertical arrow slit-like aperture, through which the machine gun was fired. The tank was also installed with smoke candle dischargers. This Panther carries a summer camouflage scheme of sand base RAL 7028 and is oversprayed across the superstructure, turret and barrel in patches of olive green RAL 6003 and brown RAL 6003. Its tactical number 632 on the turret side is painted in red with a white outline. (Tom Cooper)

Sd.Kfz.231 (8-rad) Reconnaissance Vehicle This vehicle is armed with the 2cm KwK30 and an MG34 for local fire support. The 231 was introduced into service in 1932 and began to be replaced in 1937 when the Wehrmacht began producing the eight-wheeled armored vehicles instead of the six-wheeled. The crew comprised the commander, gunner, driver, and a radio operator/rear driver. These vehicles were issued to the heavy reconnaissance detachment of the Aufkl.Abt of motorized infantry and panzer divisions to provide support for lighter armored cars. They were produced from 1936 until May 1942, but saw service during Kursk. This reconnaissance vehicle is painted in the typical sand base color and oversprayed in a camouflage color of brown RAL 6003. (Tom Cooper)

Sd.Kfz. 250/8 leichter Schützenpanzerwagen (7.5 cm) Stummel This halftrack mounted the powerful 7.5cm KwK 37 L/24 cannon. It entered service in 1943 to equip the heavy sections of the panzergrenadiers. For local defense it was also armed with the MG34 which was installed on the top of the gun. The Sd.Kfz.250 was used in a wide variety of roles on the battlefield, from a basic troop carrier to reconnaissance units carrying scout sections. This late variant was predominantly used to support infantry and tanks. It is painted in overall dark sand base RAL 7028 with mottled effect brown lines RAL 8020 across the chassis. (Tom Cooper)

Army Group Center Commanders

Hitler charged his best commanders on the Eastern Front to take command of the operations at Kursk, which he hoped would yield him victory.

Günther von Kluge

Field Marshal Günther von Kluge was one of the most notable high-ranking Prussian officers during World War II, who held important commands both of the Western and Eastern Fronts. He had been given the command of Army Group Center and was heavily involved in operations during the latter part of the battle for Moscow, and then saw extensive service during the summer offensive in 1942, and in the Third Battle for Kharkov in March 1943. Following the Kharkov operation, Kluge was authorized to take command of Army Group Center for the battle of Kursk.

Erich-Heinrich Cloessner

General Erich-Heinrich Cloessner was a prime candidate for Kursk following the replacement of Rudolf "Panzer" Schmidt. Cloessner was a very active and strong-minded panzer commander with years of military experience who had commanded at both divisional and corps levels with much success. He took charge of the Second Panzer Army at Kursk

Walther Model

General Walter Model (at left in the photograph, talking to Guderian) was an aggressive and strategic panzer commander who later became best known as a practitioner of defensive warfare. Many commanders in the field, as well as the troops, looked upon Model as the Führer's troubleshooter. Out on the battlefield Model was not only energetic, courageous and innovative, but also friendly and popular with his enlisted men. His obstinate style of fighting and devotion to the Nazi cause won him considerable praise from Hitler. It was not a surprise that Model was afforded the "honor" of commanding the Ninth Army.

Walter Weiss

General Walter-Otto Weiss was of Prussian aristocracy and quickly went through the ranks as a dedicated, loyal and determined officer. As one of the senior commanders in Operation *Barbarossa*, he soon earned the respect of his men. In July 1942, Weiss took command of XXVII Army Corps, before being given the command of the Second Army on the Eastern Front in February 1943.

The moment a *nebeltruppe* battery launches one of its deadly Nebelwerfer rockets at Soviet positions during the opening phase of *Zitadelle*. Note the distinctive smoke trails from the rockets.

infantry divisions. To the left of XLI Panzer Corps was XXIII Army Corps, which boasted two infantry divisions and was supported by the 78th Assault Infantry Division. Opposing this arsenal was the Russian Central Front, which was made up of three heavily defended defensive belts.

Along the entire front the Germans were in a high state of readiness to unleash their might against the Red Army defenses. Morale and equipment levels were reported to be

Another photograph taken during a Nebelwerfer rocket attack during the initial stages of the offensive. Although designed primarily as an anti-personnel weapon, these rockets proved lethal against open and soft-skinned vehicles.

Artillery and mortar fire pound Soviet defensive positions during the opening attack.

Taken from an artillery observation post, the sprawling countryside is dotted with artillery explosions. Armored vehicles can be made out advancing in the distance.

strong among both the panzer and infantry divisions. Most were impatient to end the months of inactivity and begin the battle upon which all their thoughts had been focused for so long. Following weeks of preparation, it was announced to the frontline command posts that *Zitadelle* would begin during the early hours of July 5. During the eve of the offensive German artillery positions began preparing for their massive preliminary bombardment in order to soften up the first enemy defensive belt to allow the panzers and then the infantry to pour through the breaches.

Units which were to form the first line of attack began drawing up toward the front lines. Nearby the assault detachments moved up and waited with anxiety at their jumping-off points. These units were composed of sappers and infantry supported by heavy machine guns, mortars, and a number of tanks and self-propelled guns. Behind the assault detachments came advanced battalions, which were heavily supported by tanks and self-propelled guns.

As the Germans completed their battle readiness, there was a general feeling, not of elation at the thought of undertaking one of the boldest attacks thus far on the Eastern Front, but something more deeply ingrained: a firm belief to do one's duty for the Fatherland and change forever their misfortunes in Russia.

The moment a powerful 21cm Mrs18 gun is fired. Note the crew blocking their ears as the blast reverberates through their position. This large-caliber gun had a range of almost 17 kilometers. Weighing 16.7 tons, it remained in service until the end of the war.

A 10.5cm leFH 16 light field howitzer in action. The wheels of this gun were of heavy-duty cast steel with a solid rubber rim. This type of design allowed the gun to be towed at relatively high speed by a motorized vehicle.

Following the massive German artillery bombardment along the Soviet front, armored vehicles followed by troops advanced against the first line of defense.

At 0430 hours it finally came, German gunners began their massive artillery bombardment. Almost immediately across vast parts of Army Group Center the front erupted in a wall of flame and smoke. Hundreds of guns and mortars and 2,000 Nebelwerfer rocket launchers poured fire and destruction onto the Russian defensive positions. Shell after shell thundered into the Soviet strongpoints. In some sectors of the front the line was totally destroyed, only to be replaced by more soldiers.

Along the whole front the German artillery devoted the majority of its time to supporting the reconnaissance attacks and pulverizing the Soviet defensive positions and destroying areas deep in the Russian lines. From the air too came the Luftwaffe, which conducted attacks against major troop concentrations and artillery positions.

The Red Army Air Force retaliated in turn, diving and bombing, as on the ground Soviet artillery simultaneously pounded the German trenches, to a depth of more than three miles in some places. The heavy artillery duel lasted between one and two hours on average, but in some areas continued for longer. The German artillery barrage was one of the largest artillery offensives of the war. In fact, the bombardment was so intense that the Germans used more shells in an hour than they had used during the entire campaigns in both Poland in 1939 and the Western Front in 1940.

A Pz.Kpfw.IV advancing across a field. In the distance village buildings are burning, evidence of artillery and tank fire. All morning on the first day of the offensive, Soviet defenses endured relentless German fire. Red Army troops were duty-bound to hold their lines on pain of death.

Infantrymen on the march during the initial phase of the offensive. The soldier on the left has an MG34 machine gun on his shoulder for ease of carriage.

Whilst the German artillery bombardment continued, Freissener's XXIII Corps, situated on the right flank of the Ninth Army, began advancing with its tanks rolling forward and infantry following closely behind. It did not take long before it became apparent that it was up against stiff opposition. However, greater success was being made in Model's advance, which had simultaneously plunged into action, hurling elements of the XLVII and XLI Panzer Corps against the enemy defenses. The 20th Panzer Division with its Pz.Kpfw.IIIs and IVs led the advance across minefields and antitank emplacements.

An infantry unit advances to the front. It would soon become apparent to the German soldier that the battle of Kursk was unlike any other engagement he had previously encountered. Resistance by the Red Army would cost the Wehrmacht dearly.

Russian PoWs being led away to an uncertain fate. During the early phase of the battle thousands of Soviet troops were killed or captured.

Laden Sd.Kfz.251 halftracks transport men to the forward edge of the battlefield. Even during the initial stages of *Zitadelle* the supply situation was exacerbated by the almost non-existence of proper roads throughout the region. Halftracks and other tracked vehicles were utilized to help speed up the transportation of soldiers, supply of ammunition and other matériel desperately required at the front.

A panzer crewman interrogates a captured Russian tanker who stands beside his knocked out-tank.

An Sd.Kfz.251 halftrack follows one of a number of Russian PoWs captured during the initial stage of the offensive. In the background German infantry escort captured Russian soldiers from their defensive positions back to the rear.

By 0900 hours the 20th Panzer Division reported it had reached the village of Bobrik before hurling its might a further three miles through stubborn Russian lines.

By late morning Tiger tanks of the vaunted 505th Heavy Tank Battalion had smashed headlong through heavy fire and entered the town of Butyrkin, sending Soviet infantrymen fleeing for their lives. Further penetrations by armor and infantry continued all morning. At Ponyri the 653rd Jagdpanzer Battalion with their bristling Ferdinands, bulldozed their way through Alexadrovka, but then ran into stiff opposition and found itself cut off from its supporting infantry and vehicles.

Around Ponyri fighting was still fierce. It was here that the Germans discovered that the Red Army was using new tactics. In previous battles the Russians had often attacked on a broad front with minimal artillery support. Now they had adopted German tactics by concentrating large numbers of infantry supported by heavy artillery and armor in their counterattacks. From various observation posts dug in along the front the Germans found that the Red Army was strong and well armed, and that their defensive positions were more robust than they had first anticipated.

However, in spite of every yard of ground being bitterly contested by the Red Army, by the end of the first day, July 5, it was reported that Model`s units west of Ponyri had pushed six miles into the first line of Soviet defenses. Although on paper the advance appeared

On the advance is an Sd.Kz.251 communications vehicle, fitted with extra radio equipment for command. The halftrack also mounts an MG34 machine and splinter shield for local defense.

Late-variant Pz.Kpfw.IIIs on the move. During the initial stages of *Barbarossa* the Pz.Kpfw.III showed its worth. However, against formidable Soviet armor such as the T-34 medium and the KV-1 heavy tanks, the Pz.Kpfw.III was soon recognized as inadequate. Note the side-skirts, or *schürzen*, protecting the wheels and the turret against antitank shells.

Panzergrendiers disembark from an Sd.Kfz.251 halftrack armored personnel carrier. This vehicle was used extensively during the war to carry troops to the forward edge of battle, where it would unload them for action.

An Sd.Kfz.10/4 armed with a 2cm FlaK 30. The side gun platform could be folded down to provide additional space for the crew to maneuver around the gun. Note the magazine boxes attached to the sides.

Soviet PoWs being escorted to the rear. Their future is bleak. Many either starved to death in hastily erected PoW camps, or were transported to Poland or Germany where they were worked to death in one of the many labor camps.

A radio vehicle has halted in a field. The men inside the car are signalmen operating a portable radio that can be seen affixed at the rear of the vehicle. These were the standard radios used at battalion and regimental level. They were often carried by a soldier on a specially designed backpack frame and, when connected to each other (upper and lower valves) via special cables, could be used on the march.

On the advance across the steppe are halftracks and other supporting vehicles in a column. The halftrack was a diverse machine and notably the Sd.Kfz.7 and 8 were used extensively, not just to carry troops to the battlefield, but to tow ordnance such as artillery and flak guns.

Halted inside a village are a number of Sd.Kfz.251 halftracks and support vehicles. An inquisitive Russian peasant watches the spectacle.

A halftrack towing a 5cm PaK 38 gun to the front. The PaK 38's effectiveness on the battlefield made it a popular weapon with both the Heer and Waffen-SS, but there were never enough of them to meet the ever-increasing demand on the Eastern Front. Throughout its life on the battlefield the PaK 38 was a deadly weapon, especially in the hands of well-trained antitank gunners.

Infantry supported by armor during a drive across the steppe. In the Kursk region the area was deemed good tank country, but did expose soldiers to hostile enemy fire.

Concealed in undergrowth is a Wespe tank destroyer. This vehicle, used extensively at Kursk, was armed with a 10.5cm leFH 18/2 L/28 gun and protected by a lightly armored superstructure mounted on a chassis of a Pz.Kpfw.II. It served in armored artillery battalions but, being lightly armored, many of its operators were lost in battle.

A Marder III crew conversing and observing a map. The upper structure of the vehicle mounted the gun; an extended gun shield only gave limited protection to the crew. Armor protection overall ranged from 10mm to 50mm thick with no armor at all above and behind the gun compartment.

successful, it came with a cost: the Germans had in fact sacrificed nearly a quarter of their men and armored vehicles. Some 20,000 soldiers had been killed, captured, or wounded, and 200 tanks and assault vehicles out of the 300 committed to battle had been captured or destroyed. Though Model remained outwardly confident in front of his men, Army Group Center had in fact taken a heavy battering.

For the next four days the Germans were compelled to fight their way along the ridges stretching between Ponyri and the villages of Olkhavatka and Samodurovka in order to try and reach the northern route to Kursk. However, the ridges themselves were impregnable fortresses, bristling as they were with various trenches, tank obstacles, and other impressive strongholds, which included dozens of reinforced machine-gun and mortar pits. The areas in front of the ridges were often heavily mined and consisted of many antitank strongpoints and a network of obstacles that were protected by extensive barbed-wire barriers. Manning these lines were well dug-in troops armed with an impressive array of weapons installed in series of machine-gun pits.

During the early hours of the second day of the offensive Model's Ninth Army attacked in a northerly direction in order to try and batter its way through the Soviet defenses. The objective was to try and break through the Red Army's Central Front's second defensive belt around the village of Ponyri and to the north of Olkhovatka.

A Tiger V belonging to the vaunted 505th Heavy Tank Battalion crossing the first defensive belt in Army Group Center. For the attack, the unit had 31 Tigers and was joined on July 9, 1943 by 3rd Company, which was formed in April and received its Tigers in June. The 505th lost only four Tigers during the Kursk offensive but was to lose a further six by the end of July 1943.

The main German force boasted some 1,000 tanks, 3,000 guns and mortars, and 5,000 machine guns. Leading the attack was the 2nd Panzer Division, to which was attached the 505th Heavy Tank Battalion. Although some units saw some success, fighting soon turned into a battle of attrition, and although the Germans showed great fortitude and determination, they were constantly hampered by heavy resistance. In fact, it was Russian artillery that stemmed most of the German attacks.

Along the front the Red Army had equipped their lines with M-30 Katyusha rocket launchers, which, up until now, had rarely been used in defensive actions. So as German armor and infantry pushed forward toward

An Ad.Kfz.10/4 mounting a 2cm flak gun rolls along a road accompanying a wheeled vehicle convoy. Although out of the frame, the vehicle is hauling an Sd.AH.51 ammunition trailer.

the ridges, the troops had to endure the "Katushkas" or "Stalin's Organs," as the soldiers called them. These weapons with their distinctive shriek fired projectiles from 16-rail rocket launchers several miles into the German lines. Although it was not a precision weapon, it was hardly necessary if 16 rockets impacted an area about the size of four football pitches, dumping more than 300 kilograms of explosives on the target. The terrifying noise they made was much feared by the Germans.

Yet, in spite the heavy artillery, the Germans rumbled forward and, following a fierce firefight, the hamlet of Soborovka was captured. Model, now more confident, ordered the 9th Panzer Division forward to reinforce his forces being battered by heavy resistance at the front. Unabated fighting continued and losses were massive as armored units slowly inched their way deeper into the web of intricate Russian defenses.

But slowly and systematically the Germans were being pulverized. Those troops fortunate enough to escape the slaughter immediately found themselves in hostile, open countryside with lurking Soviet soldiers inflicting terrible casualties on them. Repeatedly, the Tigers were moved forward to stem the killing, but the enemy drove them back.

Dug in along a railway line is a crew with their Sd.Kz.10/4 halftrack. The 2cm flak gun points in the direction of the enemy lines. An impromptu shelter has been erected between the halftrack and rail line using a *Zeltbahn* shelter quarter, which was standard issue to the infantry throughout the war.

In Profile: Panzers at *Zitadelle*

Pz.Kpfw.IV Ausf.G The production run for the Ausf.G was between May 1942 and June 1943. This variant went through a series of production modifications which included another armor upgrade. Much of the armored plate received additional thickness such as the frontal armor plates being increased to 80mm. Other modifications were also adopted, such as the vision ports on either side of the turret and on the right turret front being removed, while a rack for two spare wheels was installed on the track guard on the left side of the hull. Complementing this, brackets for seven spare track links were added to the glacis plate. For operation in high temperatures, the engine's ventilation was improved by creating slits over the engine deck to the rear of the chassis, and cold weather performance was boosted by adding a device to heat the engine's coolant, as well as a starter fluid injector. On March 19, 1943, the first Pz.Kpfw.IV with side-skirts, or *schürzen*, on its sides and turret entered service. The double hatch for the commander's cupola was replaced by a single round hatch from the very late model Ausf.G. and the cupola was uparmored as well. In April 1943, the KwK 40 L/43 was replaced by the longer 7.5cm KwK 40 L/48 gun, with a redesigned multi-baffle muzzle brake with improved recoil efficiency. The panzer has received a summer camouflage scheme of sand base color RAL 7028 with a heavy overspray of olive green RAL 6003 and red brown RAL 8017. (Tom Cooper)

Pz.Kpfw.I Ausf.F This Pz.Kpfw.I Ausf. F varied considerably from the early design with increased armor and new suspension. Its frontal armor was increased to 80mm, 50mm on the side and rear, and 25mm on the bottom and top. The interleaved wheels with torsion bar suspension and wide tracks were used to disperse its weight. As it was no match against Soviet armor, the vehicle was relegated to reconnaissance duties. In 1943 eight of these tanks were issued to the 1st Panzer Division, and three were reported to be operating with the 12th Panzer Division. At Kursk, they were rare as many were being utilized as training vehicles. (Tom Cooper)

Pz.Kpfw.IV Ausf.H During the preparation for Kursk the Panzerwaffe went through a series of drastic upgrades with their panzers, one of which included the addition of *schürzen*. Whilst this afforded protection from Soviet antitank rounds, the tanks were prone to lose some of their side-skirts either in battle or due to high wear and tear, as this profile indicates. This tank is painted in the typical standard sand base color RAL 7028 and sprayed with olive green RAL 6003 patches of the superstructure and what's left of its *schürzen*. (Tom Cooper)

Panzer III Ausf.M The Ausf.M was still armed with the 5cm KwK39 L/60, although that gun was proving to be increasingly ineffective against thicker Soviet tank armor. The variant was given 20mm spaced armor on the superstructure front and mantlet, and thicker frontal turret armor. It was very similar to the Ausf.L model, but with the addition of a wading kit which allowed it to pass through four or five feet of water without any special preparation. This example is painted in brown RAL 8020 and olive green. (Tom Cooper)

A prime mover towing a 15cm sFH 18 howitzer to the front, the standard divisional artillery piece.

Artillerymen on a halftrack. One soldier points, suggesting he suspects the location of the enemy.

A halftrack with a modified 10.5cm leFH 18/42 gun on tow has halted in a ditch. The gun crew are digging out a position for the artillery piece. The 10.5cm was the standard light artillery piece deployed in the artillery divisions on the Eastern Front. However, in order to give the gun better punch on the battlefield the weapon was modified in 1942: the barrel was lengthened, a cage muzzle brake was fitted, and the carriage was a lightened version of the leFH 18 design.

A German soldier stands next to a knocked-out Soviet T-34 tank. Dead crewmen are scattered around the vehicle.

One of the most impressive mortars used by the Germans at Kursk was the 12cm Granatwerfer 378(r), as seen being prepared for a fire mission in the summer of 1943. The weapon, weighing 285kg, consisted of a circular base plate, the tube and the supporting bipod. Because of its excessive weight, a two-wheeled axle was utilized, enabling the mortar to be towed into action. The axle could then be quickly removed before firing. The weapon fired the Wurfgranate 42 round, which carried 3.1kg of explosive.

Various armored vehicles are purposely spread out across the steppe to present a more difficult target. This was common practice by the Germans and it became standard practice during the Kursk offensive.

Two Sd.Kfz.223 (4-rad) armored scout cars advancing along a road. These vehicles were used extensively at Kursk and were generally attached to the armored brigades' reconnaissance companies.

Elsewhere in Army Group Center the fighting intensified as the Russians exploited the receding front by methodically reducing the German offensive. The Soviet counterattacks were immense, ferocious, and without respite. After three long days of almost continuous battle, the German soldier was exhausted and fighting for his very survival in a number of places. Hitler's insistence that his troops must fight on without any tactical retreat caused many units to become encircled by Red Army rifle divisions. Out of desperation, the 216th Panzer Battalion, which provided mobile heavy artillery support, hastily deployed their "Grizzly Bears," but the German advance still faltered in spite their best efforts to advance along the northern shoulder of the Kursk salient. German infantry also found themselves exposed to hostile fire as many of their supporting tanks and assault guns were knocked out, their tracks torn off by mines or disabled by antitank fire.

Three photographs taken in sequence show the Marder II. There were two versions: the first mounted modified Soviet 7.62cm guns firing German ammunition, while the other mounted the powerful German 7.5cm PaK 40 gun. Whilst these machines offered little protection to the crew, they added significant firepower. However, the Marder was more of a gun carriage than a panzerjäger proper that could exchange shells with enemy tanks. Nevertheless, they undertook sterling service at Kursk in spite of significant losses.

Over the next few days the battle of Ponyri waged with unabated ferocity. Model knew the crucial importance of the town with its main road and rail network linking with Kursk itself. German units continued to demonstrate their ability to attack the most hazardous positions against well-prepared, dug-in enemy forces. German infantry divisions bitterly contested large areas of the countryside. Fighting was often savage, resulting in terrible casualties on both sides.

Whilst the fighting intensified around Ponyri, Model, eager to reduce the pressure around that sector, ordered the 2nd Panzer Division with the Tigers of the 505th Heavy Tank Battalion and the 20th Panzer Division to press their collective armored might against Samodurovka and Olkhovatka. This was the area where the second Soviet defensive belt began and was held by the Soviet 30th Army. Almost immediately, German tank units with infantry following closely behind rolled forward, but once again they came up against stiff opposition. Fighting was so severe that the German lines were pierced in numerous places and although considerable numbers of troops were trying to hold their positions, they were unable to avoid the encirclements that followed. Across the rolling fields and forests Tigers, Ferdinands, StuG.IIIs, Pz.Kpfw.IIIs, and IVs were seen clashing with Russian defenses and T-34 tanks, whilst the infantry fought desperately against an enemy with seemingly limitless resources.

By July 11, desperate measures by Model were played out in and around Ponyri as the 10th Panzergrenadier Division launched a series of desperate attacks to hold the town. Outside the town German tanks in groups of 60 to 100, supported by infantry and assault guns from the 2nd, 4th, and 20th Panzer Divisions, made one last frantic drive against the ridge north of Olkhovatka. The wreckage of previous failed attacks was evident with

A photograph taken from a Pz.Kpfw.IV that shows its 7.5cm gun barrel. Despite the Panzerwaffe's impressive array of firepower at Kursk, there was still a shortage of infantry, which consequently led to panzer units being required to take on more ambitious tasks normally preserved for the infantry.

charred hulks still smoking as Model's tank units rolled forward. In front of them was a heavily defended labyrinth of trenches, barbed wire, mines, antitank emplacements, and well-armed infantry.

As the tank armada moved forward, exposed German infantrymen were cut to pieces by machine-gun fire. Simultaneously, the panzers were subjected to a hurricane of unceasing fire. What followed was utter confusion as tank crews were seen either trying to withdraw from the battle zone or were killed jumping from their blazing vehicles. If this was not enough, for hours German troops were subjected to merciless low-level Soviet fighter-bomber attacks, all the while being blasted by artillery. In a desperate attempt to survive, German troops hastily dug foxholes and trenches to try and protect themselves from the incessant shelling. The chaos was so all-encompassing that German officers arriving to take over units soon discovered nothing to take over, because their commands had already been captured or annihilated. In most areas well-armed soldiers were left leaderless, with no idea where they were or who was fighting on their flanks.

Whilst some areas still held fanatically, a general breakdown began to envelop the lines. Both German infantry and tank crews were completely stunned by the sheer force of the blow that had hit Army Group Center. After more than a week of fighting the battlefield was wrought with death and destruction. Although the Panzerwaffe was generally as determined as ever to fight on, they were constantly being isolated and trapped by superior numbers of enemy infantry. Areas still in German hands were slowly reduced to a few shrinking pockets of resistance.

As a result of the dire situation and to avert the total catastrophic destruction of Army Group Center, Model pulled his units back, forced to maintain the defensive until the situation was rectified. He hoped that the southern thrust would draw off heavy pressure in the north and allow his forces to renew their offensive and take Kursk.

A column of prime movers towing camouflaged 15cm howitzers towards the front. This particular gun was primarily designed to attack targets deep in the enemy's rear which included command posts, reserve units, assembly areas, and logistics facilities.

Units begin to advance towards the first defensive belt following a massive artillery bombardment on Red Army defensive positions. Here panzergrenadiers have halted near a road with two stationary Sd.Kfz.251 halftracks. The Panzerwaffe relied heavily on the various light and heavy armored vehicles for transportation. Maintaining the momentum of an advance was vital to the success of an offensive.

Army Group South

In the south, German Army Group South prepared its lines for attack. For the offensive the army group boasted the powerful Fourth Panzer Army and Army Detachment Kempf. On the western side of the salient was positioned the Second Army. Army Group South was equipped with more armored vehicles, infantry, and artillery than Army Group Center. The Fourth Panzer Army, which included the cream of the Waffen-SS panzer divisions, and Army Detachment Kempf had some 1,377 tanks and assault guns.

Order of Battle, July 1943

ARMY GROUP SOUTH (Erich von Manstein)

FOURTH PANZER ARMY (Hermann Hoth)
<u>LII Corps (E. Ott)</u>

57th Infantry Division
255th Infantry Division
332nd Infantry Division

<u>XLVIII Panzer Corps (O. von Knobelsdorff)</u>

3rd Panzer Division
11th Panzer Division
Panzergrenadier Division Grossdeutschland
167th Infantry Division
II SS Panzer Corps (P. Hausser)
1st SS Panzergrenadier Division Leibstandarte SS Adolf Hitler
2nd SS Panzergrenadier Division Das Reich
3rd SS Panzergrenadier Division Totenkopf

ARMY GROUP KEMPF (W. Kempf)
<u>III Panzer Corps (H. Breith)</u>

6th Panzer Division
7th Panzer Division
19th Panzer Division
168th Infantry Division
Raus' Corps (E. Raus)
106th Infantry Division
320th Infantry Division

<u>XLII Corps (F. Mattenklott)</u>

39th Infantry Division
161st Infantry Division
282nd Infantry Division

ARMY GROUP RESERVE
<u>XXIV Panzer Corps (W. Nehring)</u>

5th SS Panzergrenadier Division Wiking
17th Panzer Division

LUFTWAFFE
Luftflotte 4 (4th Air Fleet)
VIII Air Corps
Luftflotte 6
1st Air Division

In Profile:
German self-propelled guns and half-tracks

Nashorn 8.8cm Pak 43 (L/71) auf Geschützwagen III/IV Sd. Kfz. 164 Known as the Nashorn, or rhinoceros, but initially nicknamed as the Hornisse or hornet, the Nashorn looked similar to the Hummel, but unlike the Hummel this light turretless vehicle mounted a very lethal PaK 43 heavy antitank gun. The Nashorn entered production in early 1943, and during this period of transformation it was given numerous official designations, such as 8.8cm Pak 43 (L/71) auf Fahrgestell Panzerkampfwagen III/IV (Sf) or 8.8cm PaK 43 (L/71) auf Geschützwagen III/IV (Sd. Kfz. 164); it was also designated as a Panzerjäger Hornisse. Much hope hinged on the success of these new modified vehicles to support the panzer and infantry during the German summer offensive in 1943. By this period the Panzerwaffe fielded some 24 panzer divisions on the Eastern Front alone. This was a staggering transformation of a panzer force that had lost immeasurable amounts of armor in less than two years of combat. This vehicle has been painted in a dark yellow sand base RAL 7028 with a camouflage scheme of wavy horizontal lines, large brown lines RAL 8020 across its superstructure and along its barrel. (Tom Cooper)

Panzerjäger Tiger "Ferdinand" Elefant Sd.Kfz.184 Pzabt 654 A number of new vehicles were to make their debut in the Kursk operation and the manufacturers were eager to see their success. Another tank hunter to join the armored might of the Panzerwaffe in that summer was a vehicle named the Elefant or elephant. This was a heavy tank destroyer like no other during this time. It was built in small numbers under the name Ferdinand after its designer Ferdinand Porsche, using hulls that had been produced for the mighty Tiger I. The Elefant was fitted with the powerful 8.8cm Panzerjägerkanone 43/2 gun (early designation 8.8cm Stu.K. 43/1). Ninety-one of these panzerjägers were produced by May 1943, with 89 committed to the Kursk operation. This vehicle is painted in a sand base color with green RAL 6003 and brown stripes RAL 6003. (Tom Cooper)

Panzerfeldhaubitze 18M auf Geschützwagen III/IV (Sf) Hummel, Sd.Kfz. 165 The Hummel, or bumblebee, was a gun adapted and mounted on the Geschützwagen III/IV chassis and armed with a 15cm howitzer. This Panzerfeldhaubitze 18M auf Geschützwagen III/IV (Sf) Hummel, Sd.Kfz. 165 entered service in 1943. Initially, designers had wanted to mount a 10.5cm leFH 18 howitzer on the chassis of a Pz.Kpfw.III, but it was rejected in favor of the more powerful and larger Pz.Kpfw.IV chassis. As with all the self-propelled artillery vehicles, they were produced with a lightly armored open top that housed the gun and the crew. The engine was moved to the center of the vehicle to make additional space in the fighting compartment. When the Hummel came off the production line in the first half of 1943 it was tested and put through its paces, and then signed off. It made its debut at Kursk in July 1943 with some 100 Hummels in service. These vehicles served in the armored artillery battalions, or *panzerartillerie abteilungen*, of the panzer divisions, forming separate heavy self-propelled artillery batteries, each with six Hummels and one ammunition carrier. This particular Hummel from an unidentified *panzerartillerie abteilung* is painted in a standard gray base color RAL 7021 with green streaky lines RAL 6003 across the vehicle's superstructure and barrel.

Marder II Ausf.E The Marder was based on the chassis of the Pz.Kpfw.II. There were two versions: the first mounted modified Soviet 7.62cm guns firing German ammunition, while the other mounted the powerful German 7.5cm PaK 40 gun. This vehicle was designed with a high profile and open-topped armor with minimal protection for the crew. This example has been painted in a sand base RAL 7028 with brown RAL 8020 and olive green RAL 6003 stripes over the chassis, open turret compartment and gun barrel. (Tom Cooper)

Army Group South Commanders

Army Group South commanders boasted a host of very experienced, dedicated and proficient officers to plan and execute the offensive.

Erich von Manstein

Field Marshal Erich von Manstein (pictured left) was born into an aristocratic Prussian family with a long tradition of military service. On the Eastern Front he saw extensive service in Crimea and at the battle of Sevastopol, siege of Leningrad, battle of Stalingrad, and the Kharkov counteroffensive, before becoming commander of the Ninth Army at Kursk. It was Manstein who favored an immediate pincer attack on the Kursk salient after the battle at Kharkov, but Hitler was concerned that such a plan would draw off important panzer and infantry forces from the industrial region of the Donets Basin.

Herman Hoth

General Hermann Hoth (pictured right) was an aristocratic Prussian officer who commanded the Fourth Panzer Army at Kursk. As a very able and competent panzer commander and responsible for a series of impressive successes on the Eastern Front, for the offensive he was rewarded with command of the Fourth Panzer Army.

Werner Kempf

General Werner Kempf was a well-known panzer commander who brought much experience to the strategic planning at Kursk. For the offensive he commanded Army Detachment Kempf, which had previously fought successfully at the Third Battle for Kharkov between February and March 1943.

Walter Nehring

General Walter Nehring was a Prussian officer with a successful career as a panzer commander. He had taken command of the Afrika Korps in May 1942 and took part in the last major Axis offensive of the Western Desert. Following operations in North Africa, Nehring was posted to the Eastern Front where he would excel as commander of the XXIV Panzer Corps at Kursk.

An 8.8cm Flak gun belonging the SS Leibstandarte, seen here in an antiaircraft role.

The Battle

During the early hours of July 5, the morning was suddenly broken by the shouts of German gunnery officers giving the order for their men to commence a large artillery barrage against Soviet defenses on the Southern Front. For almost 90 minutes German artillery pounded the enemy, engulfing Red Army positions in a sea of fire and explosion. Once the bombardments dissipated, armored vehicles from Army Detachment Kempf and Hoth's Fourth Panzer Army began their attack. Their main objective was to seize the bridgeheads over the River Psel, south of Oboyan.

In order to achieve their objective the II SS Panzer Corps and the XLVIII Panzer Corps rolled along two converging roads toward the towns of Oboyan and Pokrovka. The center of the thrust was undertaken by the Grossdeutschland Panzergrenadier Division supported by tanks of the 3rd and 11th Panzer Divisions. Supporting the armor were the 167th and 332nd Infantry Divisions. Among the panzers the XLVIII Panzer Corps boasted the new Panther tanks. However, their debut got off to a bad start. As they rolled forward they ran into a large minefield near Butovo with some of them grounding to a flaming halt in the boggy ravines. This led to confusion among the Panther crews and as they tried to extricate themselves they set off more mines. Chaos ensued, and as a result 36 Panthers were lost.

A relief operation was immediately put into action to try and relieve the remaining stricken Panthers stuck in the boggy minefield. The 11th Panzer Division launched a series of powerful drives, smashing through Soviet defenses and rolling into the smoldering village of Cherkasskoe, from where the Panthers could be pulled out.

Photographed from a moving Pz.Kpfw.IV, the vehicle is following a number of other armored vehicles spread out across the steppe during the initial stages of the attack.

On the advance: a number of armored vehicles can be seen during the early part of the offensive. The vehicle nearest the camera is a Pz.Kpfw.IV: Panzer 4 of the 6th Company of the 3rd SS Panzer Regiment of the Totenkopf Division. Note the Roman III painted in yellow on the vehicle's left front indicating it is attached to the Totenkopf.

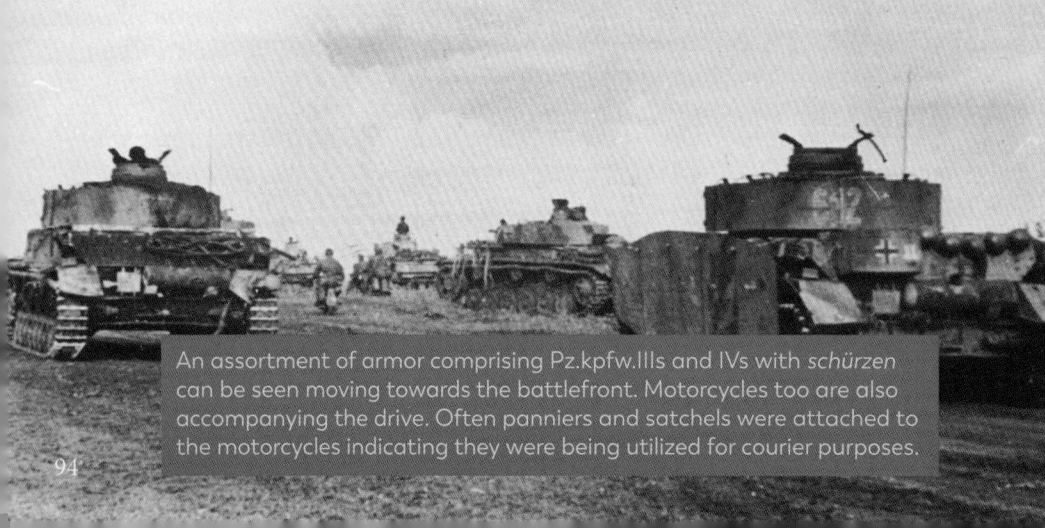

An assortment of armor comprising Pz.kpfw.IIIs and IVs with *schürzen* can be seen moving towards the battlefront. Motorcycles too are also accompanying the drive. Often panniers and satchels were attached to the motorcycles indicating they were being utilized for courier purposes.

Yet, in spite of the successful relief operation, the tanks once again stalled in front of the stiff lines of countless antitank positions and heavy artillery fire. Undeterred, the panzers of Grossdeutschland's Tiger company pressed on through the ferocious shelling, bulldozing their way forward and allowing supporting grenadiers to take up better positions.

Meanwhile, Hausser's II SS Panzer Corps demonstrated its skill and tenacity associated with that of the fighting élan of the Waffen-SS units. Hausser's corps comprised the three premier Waffen-SS divisions: 1st SS Panzer Division Leibstandarte Adolf Hitler, the 2nd SS Division Das Reich, and the 3rd SS Panzer Division Totenkopf. These three divisions had a line strength of 390 of the latest tanks and 104 assault guns between them, including 42 of the Army Group South's Tigers. At their starting positions, the three SS divisions covered a sector some 12 miles wide. The Totenkopf occupied the left flank of the advance, the Leibstandarte the center, and Das Reich held the right. With a remarkable combination of speed and concentrated firepower the Waffen-SS divisions pushed forward with all fury toward Bykovka.

The initial stages of Hausser's attack went well with advanced SS units encircling Red Army soldiers and destroying them with supporting grenadiers. The 9th Company of the Leibstandarte's 2nd SS Panzergrenadier Regiment captured two hills west of Byelgorod and took five fortified positions with explosive charges. Simultaneously, soldiers of the vaunted Totenkopf division with its new Tigers smashed into a series of strongly fortified defensive enemy lines, whilst the Das Reich division rolled forward and immediately became entangled in a series of clashes with Russian antitank gunners.

Throughout the day fighting raged, with the Waffen-SS seeing considerable success. In fact, by nightfall, leading units of the Totenkopf reported it had managed to reach the second defensive belt some 13 miles into the Soviet defense-in-depth, capturing the village of Yakhontovo.

Tiger tanks belonging to 505th Heavy Tank Battalion can be seen moving through a village supported by Waffen-SS troops clad in their distinctive summer camouflage smocks and helmet covers.

SS panzergrenadiers, identified by the characteristic patterns of their camouflage smocks, cross a field along with armored vehicles, including an Sd.Kfz.251, that are spread out as far as the eye can see.

A Pz.Kpfw.IV Ausf.G has halted in a village. This vehicle appears to have been back-fitted with turret and hull *schürzen* and has a summer camouflage scheme of either green or brown applied over the chassis including the spare track links that have been bolted to the front.

Waffen-SS Order of Battle at Kursk

II SS PANZER CORPS (SS-Obergruppenführer Paul Hausser)

<u>1st SS Panzer Division Leibstandarte Adolf Hitler (SS-Brigadeführer Wisch)</u>

1st SS Panzer Regiment
1st SS Panzergrenadier Regiment
2nd SS Panzergrenadier Regiment
1st SS Panzer Artillery Regiment
1st SS Panzer Reconnaissance Battalion
1st SS Panzer Engineer Battalion
1st SS Flak Battalion
Strength: 106 tanks, 35 assault guns

<u>2nd SS Panzer Division Das Reich (SS-Grupppenführer Kruger)</u>

2nd SS Panzer Regiment
3rd SS Panzergrenadier Regiment Deutschland
4th SS Panzergrenadier Regiment Der Führer
2nd SS Panzer Artillery Regiment
2nd SS Panzer Reconnaissance Battalion
2nd SS Panzer Engineer Battalion
2nd SS Flak Battalion
Strength: 145 tanks, 34 assault guns

<u>3rd SS Panzer Division Totenkopf (SS-Brigadeführer Priess)</u>

3rd SS Panzer Regiment
5th SS Panzergrenadier Regiment Thule
6th SS Panzergrenadier Regiment Theodor Eicke
3rd SS Panzer Artillery Regiment
3rd SS Panzer Reconnaissance Battalion
3rd SS Panzer Engineer Battalion
3rd SS Flak Battalion
Strength: 139 tanks, 35 assault guns

<u>122nd Artillery Command (Arko)</u>

1st Field Howitzer Detachment
1st Werfer Lehr Regiment
3rd Smoke Troop
55th Werfer Regiment
680th Pioneer Regiment
627th Poineer Battalion (mot)
666th Pioneer Battalion (mot)
861st Artillery Regiment (mot)
818th Artillery Regiment (mot)
Strength: 390 tanks, 104 assault guns

In Profile:
Panzerkampfwagen VI Tiger Ausf.E

This panzer was regarded as the backbone of the Panzerwaffe at Kursk. Although the Tiger I was well built and strongly armed, the building of it was expensive, using labor-intensive production methods. It also had track problems, limited range, and a high fuel consumption. However, in spite this, the vehicle was generally mechanically reliable, powerful, and successful against the ever-growing might of Soviet armor. The Tiger had an impressive frontal hull armor 100mm thick, frontal turret armor of 100mm, and a 120mm-thick gun mantlet, making it very difficult to knock it out by both antitank and tank rounds. It was armed with a powerful 56-caliber long 8.8cm KwK 36. This particular Tiger from the Grossdeutschland Panzergrendier Division attached to the 2nd SS Panzer Division Das Reich has a camouflage scheme of dark sand base RAL 7028 with stripes of olive green RAL 6003 and brown RAL 6003. (Tom Cooper)

Tigers were employed in separate heavy tank battalions or *schwere panzer-abteilung* under army command. These battalions were deployed to vital areas of importance on the battlefield, tasked with either breakthrough operations or counterattacking. These vehicles undertook outstanding service at Kursk and operated with only a few favored divisions, such as the Grossdeutschland and the 1st SS Panzer Division Leibstandarte Adolf Hitler, 2nd SS Panzer Division Das Reich, and 3rd SS Panzer Division Totenkopf. This particular Tiger from the Totenkopf has been painted in overall dark sand base RAL 7028 with stripes of olive green RAL 6003. In order to break up its distinctive shape on the battlefield, the crew of this particular Tiger have draped camouflage netting over the frontal part of the tank including its 8.8cm barrel. (Tom Cooper)

Sd.Kfz.231 (8-rad) Reconnaissance Vehicle

This Sd.Kfz.231 (8-rad) belongs to the Wiking Division. A heavy reconnaissance vehicle, its all-round independent steering wheels gave the machine unprecedented levels of maneuverability on all kinds of terrain and was perfect for the Kursk offensive. The vehicle is fitted with the cast visors on the turret and has the armored cowl on the rear to protect the radiator. It is painted in an overall sand base color with mottled dark gray 7021 sprayed over its armored chassis. (Tom Cooper)

StuG.III Ausf.G

The StuG.III Ausf.G was the final production version of the StuG. With a total of 7,720 built from new between December 1942 and the end of the war, it was produced in larger numbers than any other version of any German tank. It featured an improved superstructure with sloped side armor, with a commander's cupola added to the top of the fighting compartment. This vehicle has been painted in a dark yellow sand base RAL 7028 with a camouflage scheme of large brown patches RAL 8020 over its superstructure and *schürzen*. (Tom Cooper)

Two photographs showing both sides of the same tank. These images are more than likely stills from a propaganda company. These late-variant Pz.Kpfw.IVs with the tactical number 420 in white on its spaced turret plates wear the divisional insignia of the "Berlin Bear," which is always associated with the 3rd Panzer Division. Yet, the second photo clearly shows the yellow "man rune" of the 4th Panzer Division left of the front machine gun. This variation suggests that the men had transferred from the 4th to the 3rd Panzer Division and were actually commemorating their old unit.

A PzKpfw.IV in a field with panzergrenadiers hitching a ride. The vehicle's camouflage is painted in dark yellow sand base with swirls of olive-green or red-brown lines over both the body and the *schürzen*.

Waffen-SS troops are seen rounding up captured Soviet troops in a field. Almost as soon as *Zitadelle* was unleashed, the Waffen-SS drive was so rapid that thousands of Russian soldiers were encircled, captured or destroyed. However, as the Germans drove deeper into the Soviet heartland, resistance grew and the advance in several areas faltered significantly with some serious losses to men and equipment.

A troop leader armed with an MP40 machine pistol and wearing the waterproof *Zeltbahn* shelter quarter captures Russian troops in a slit trench. In the distance German armor can be seen spread out on the advance.

The following day, July 7, the SS panzer corps continued to push forward, clashing with Russian armor whilst its grenadiers fought heavy battles against determined Red Army troops. By the end of the day, Totenkopf had managed to claw its way through stiff resistance with its Tigers and Pz.Kpfw.IVs, advancing some 30 miles through heavily fortified Russian lines.

The Leibstandarte and Das Reich were similarly successful despite experiencing bitter fighting. To the SS tank crews it seemed that victory was pending, and yet, unbeknown to them, they had not even reached the principal Soviet defensive belts. The SS units had in fact been lured deep into the enemy lines where the Red Army hoped they would surround and destroy them. In spite of the danger of being cut off and surrounded, their armor and supporting grenadiers pushed slowly forward toward the town of Beregovoy with Das Reich guarding the eastern flank of the Leibstandarte and Totenkopf.

To the south other German units were also reporting relatively good progress, bringing an air of confidence into Army Group South. Army Detachment Kempf had advanced well out of its bridgehead over the River Northern Donets, while advanced units of the 6th, 7th, and 19th Panzer Divisions fought a series of successful engagements, which saw the 19th Panzer Division capturing Belovskoe.

It appeared that Kempf's tanks were having the same good fortune as Hausser's. Across the sprawling fields, hills, and ridges of the salient German tank crews observed Russian soldiers withdrawing under their relentless fire. Grossdeutschland took advantage of the retreating enemy and advanced at speed with their Panthers to try and destroy the enemy in the surrounding hills. However, as its armor moved forward, it suddenly became entangled in a minefield which had not been identified. What followed was chaos and confusion as both panzers and panzergrenadiers were sucked into several unremitting Soviet counterattacks which cost the Grossdeutschland a number of Panther losses.

In spite of the losses, Grossdeutschland had only two choices–push forward, or face annihilation in the hills. Heavy battles continued to rage, some with heavy close-

Waffen-SS troops sitting in a typical Russian slit trench. In front of them are a number of knocked-out Russian tanks. The fury of the Waffen-SS drive through the first Soviet defensive belt was undertaken successfully, and it appeared initially that the Russian forces would be destroyed.

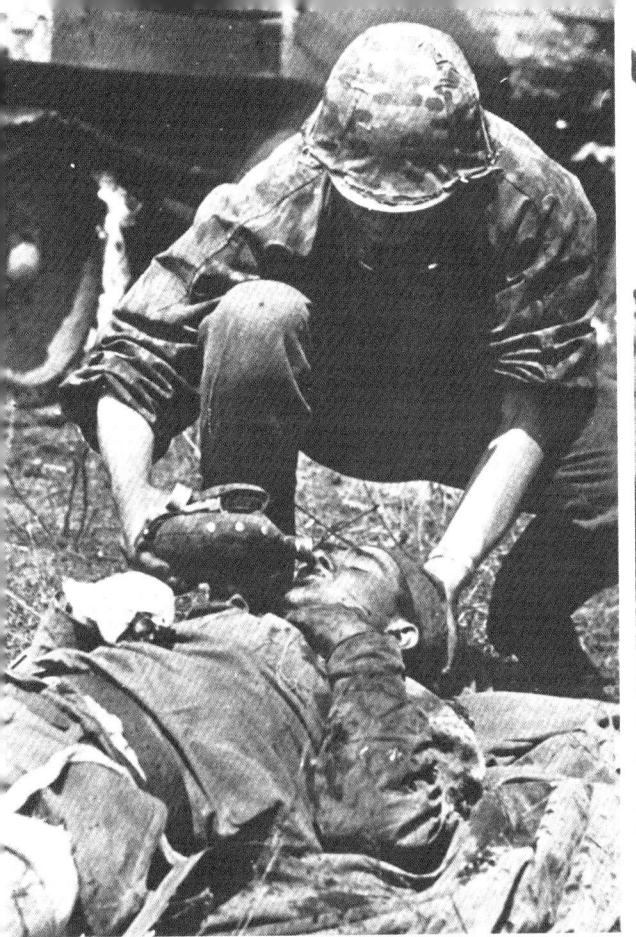

Two photographs taken in sequence showing a rare scene of Waffen-SS troops aiding captured Soviet soldiers following the destruction of their unit. A wounded Russian soldier is given a drink from an SS trooper's canteen. The second photograph shows an SS soldier, most likely from the Das Reich and armed with the standard issue Karbiner 98K bolt action rifle, conversing with a captured soldier who is assisting his comrade.

In his familiar black Panzerwaffe uniform a crewmember of the new Panther V converses with his unit commander.

In Profile:
Panther V Ausf.D Sd.Kfz. 171

The Panther made its debut on the Eastern Front at Kursk in July 1943, rushed into battle before it was fully combat-ready. Its main armament was the 7.5cm KwK42 (L/70) with semi-automatic shell ejection. At Kursk it was regarded as was one of the most powerful tanks on the battlefield, due to the large propellant charge and long barrel, which gave it a very high muzzle velocity and armor-piercing capabilities. This particular variant has been painted in typical sand base RAL 7028 and oversprayed in areas in dark brown. (Tom Cooper)

An *unteroffizier* (NCO) from the 13th Company, Grossdeutschland Panzergrenadier Regiment, Grossdeutschland Division, that was equipped with Tiger I tanks at Kursk. (Tom Cooper)

An SS soldier sleeps with his head resting on a Teller mine. This dish- or plate-shaped mine was encased with explosives sealed inside a sheet metal casing and fitted with a pressure-actuated fuse; it had a built-in carrying handle on the side. Millions were made during the war.

quarter fighting. A number of tanks, including six Tigers, were lost but the Germans were unwavering, and as a result of their robust attacks the town of Sirtsev fell, sending Russian tanks and soldiers fleeing for their lives. Further advances were made which saw advanced German units reaching the River Pena, and then undertaking clearing operations of the area to rid the fields and surrounding villages of Soviet defensive positions.

In other areas of Army Group South, reports were still confirming that the group was progressing well along several sectors of the front, in spite of stiffer resistance. Hausser's II SS

Tiger tank S14 of the Heavy Panzer Company, 2nd SS Panzer Regiment of the Das Reich rolls into action with SS panzergrenadiers following on foot. SS panzer and panzergrenadier divisions had become known as the "fire brigade" of the Third Reich. Wherever they were committed to battle they attacked.

Two photographs taken in sequence showing SS panzergrenadiers of the Das Reich supported by Tiger tanks. Although their advance had been relatively successful, it was slower than planned. In spite of this, the division had wrenched open the first defensive belt and advanced southeastward. By July 10, Das Reich had reached the Prokhorovka road where it bisected the railway line towards Storozhevka where units were to encounter unrelenting resistance.

Panzer Corps boasted it had knocked out 121 Soviet tanks on July 8, and had linked up with the XLVIII Panzer Corps at Sukho-Solotino. The 6th Panzer Division had also seen success and had advanced almost five miles in a day to reach the key road junction at Melikhovo, east of the River Lipovyi Donets.

However, in spite of Grossdeutschland's successful drive, supported by the 3rd and 11th Panzer Divisions, it was becoming more apparent that the deeper the Germans pushed east, the more resilient the Soviets became. As a result, some panzer units started to become more heavily embroiled in bitter combat and had to fiercely contest every yard of ground, with serious losses. Along some sectors of the front the battle lines blurred and then stagnated. It appeared that all hopes of wrenching open the front at Kursk now rested on the II SS Panzer Corps.

On July 9, the bulk of the II SS Panzer Corps, comprising the Leibstandarte and Totenkopf, reported it had reached the banks of the River Psel and captured the village of Krasni Oktiabr. The Leibstandarte then linked up with the 11th Panzer Division, crossed the River Solotinka and rolled forward, halting in front of the town of Kochetovka, which was heavily defended by the Soviet Independent 10th Tank Corps.

On the eastern flank of the SS spearhead Das Reich reported it had reached the Prokhorovka road and then ground to a halt before launching a number of heavy attacks in order to try and batter its way forward. During the attack Das Reich managed to inch forward along the road and partly capture the village of Ivanovskii Vyselok. Once again, SS armor and panzergrenadiers were blunted by heavy Russian resistance.

Progress was painfully slow, but *Zitadelle* would not be called off as Hitler

Pz.Kpfw.IV tanks of the Totenkopf negotiate a steep gradient during the advance. The Totenkopf covered the advance on the II SS Panzer Corps' left flank, with the Leibstandarte forming the spearhead.

A Tiger tank belonging to the 3rd SS Panzer Regiment of the Totenkopf Division. Totenkopf initially made good progress and smashed its way through the Soviet lines, over 12 miles in depth against the 52nd Guards Rifle Division. By the end of the second day, the division had penetrated some 20 miles through Red Army defenses.

SS panzergrenadiers can be seen next to a burning Russian T-34 tank. In spite of the exceptional fighting skills of the Waffen-SS, by July 9, the II SS Panzer Corps had been blunted by the tenacity of the Red Army defenders. The SS suffered horrific casualties as the offensive continued.

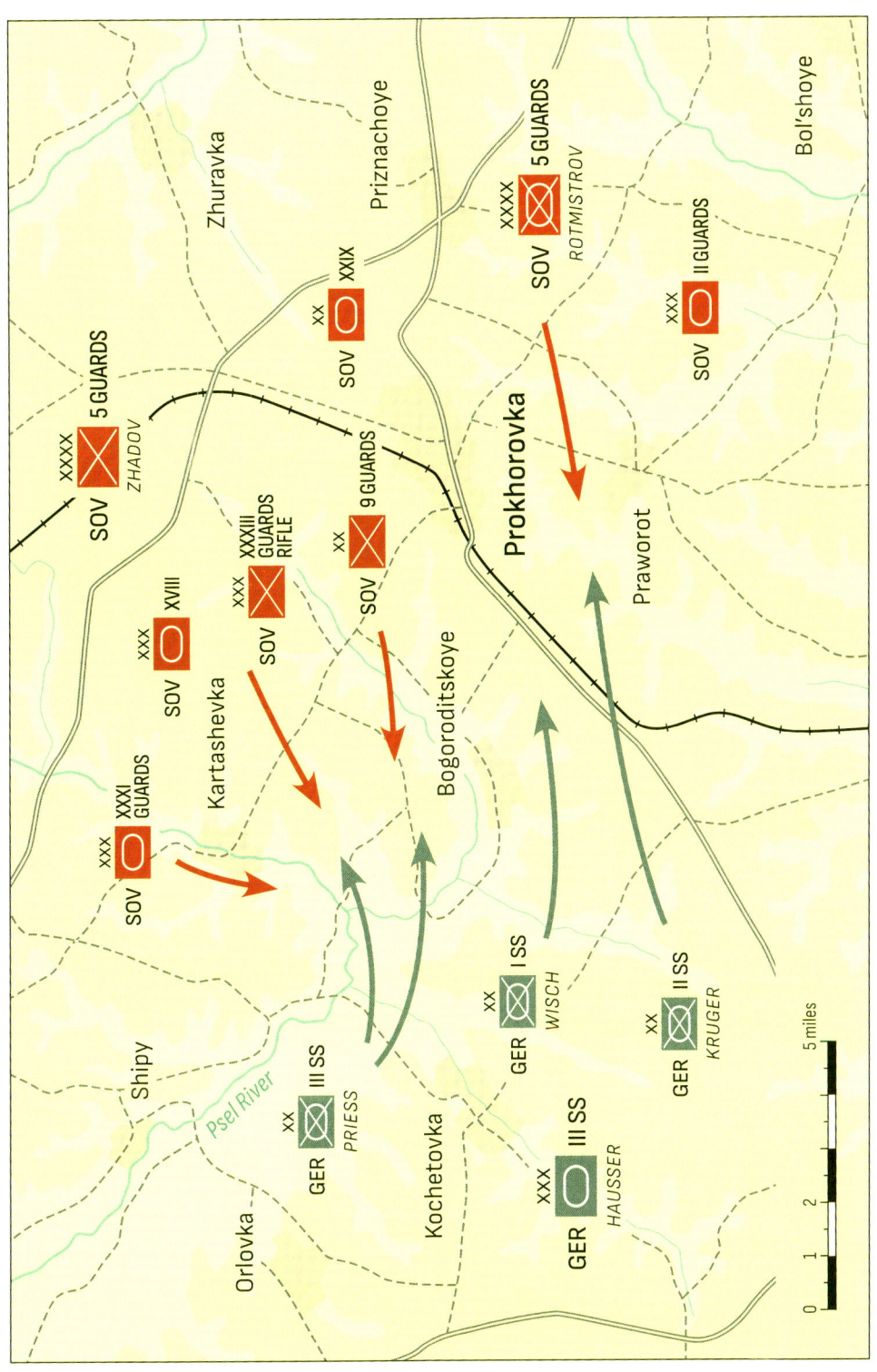

The battle of Prokhorovka opened on July 12 with the might of the II SS Panzer Corps advancing in tight formation toward Prokhorovka. The city and surrounding areas were heavily defended by Rotmistrov's 5th Tank Guards. What followed was one of the largest tank battles in military history across the fields and ridges around Bogoroditskoye and Prokhorovka.

Kursk 1943

An interesting photograph showing Russian troops using a British universal carrier for reconnaissance duties. These vehicles were open-topped and mounted an antitank rifle. The officer standing next to one of these antiquated machines is conversing with an infantryman.

Photographed near Belgorod, it appears a Tiger V crewman is about to set fire to a thatched roof. This Tiger belongs to the 503rd Heavy Panzer Battalion that was equipped with both Tiger Is and Pz.Kpfw.IIIs. Just prior to the offensive, the battalion reported that 42 of their 45 Tiger tanks were operational.

At a forward command post are two command Pz.Kpfw.IIIs complete with turret and side-plate *schürzen* and full summer camouflage markings. The motorcycles are likely part of a messenger platoon.

A Waffen-SS soldier surveys a knocked-out Soviet T-34 tank along a decimated Russian defensive position. Behind him is a Wespe tank destroyer with its crew inside its lightly armored open-topped superstructure.

A Marder III moving across a field behind a 10.5cm artillery battery.

An MG gun troop was normally a three-man squad as in this photograph, but due to high casualty rates suffered on the Eastern Front it was often reduced to two, but was still highly effective. Note the men resting inside the vehicle with a mounted MG42 machine gun.

deemed that Hausser's men had not pushed far enough ahead. News of the Führer's insistence to continue the battle brought about an ever-increasing need for the commanders to register a quick victory.

Out in the field, Hausser was determined to do his utmost to give Hitler success, but he knew it would cost him dearly. On July 11 tanks of the Leibstandarte, supported by Luftwaffe dive-bombers directed to blaze open a passage into the Soviet defense, advanced along both sides of the Prokhorovka road. What followed was a three-hour gauntlet of fire as Tiger tanks, assault guns and panzergrenadiers fought through a violent deluge of rockets, shells and bombs by formations of the 5th Guards Army. Yet, in spite of the heavy Red Army resistance, the Waffen-SS made good progress, but it did not come without significant loss in men and equipment. The armored strength of the Leibstandarte had taken the brunt of the Soviet fury and its numbers had been reduced to 10 assault guns, 60 tanks, and 20 self-propelled tank destroyers.

The losses, however, did not deter Hausser or his men. They were now supported by Army Detachment Kempf's III Panzer Corps, which was responsible for trying to divert as much attention from the main SS flanks tasked with capturing Prokhorovka as possible. The combined strength of Leibstandarte, Das Reich, and Totenkopf totaled some 77,000 men, and 122 tanks and assault guns at this time.

At dawn on July 12 elements of Leibstandarte's 1st SS Panzergrenadier Regiment rolled forward and began attacking Soviet infantry out of the village of Storozhevoe, while parts of the division's 2nd SS Panzergrenadier Regiment advanced at speed from the Oktyabrsky State

A Waffen-SS MG42 machine gunner covers a destroyed enemy position, his gun on bipods.

A Tiger crew loading up their Tiger tank with shells. Almost as soon as *Zitadelle* began, Tiger crews found that ammunition storage for the main gun was a weak point in the vehicle: all the ammunition for the main armament was stored in the hull, making the vehicle uncomfortably cramped for the crew.

Bound for the front, a Nashorn advances through a Russian town. The high profile of the Nashorn made it hard to conceal, but its long-range gun was superior to those of other tank destroyers in this period of the war.

Farm. In front of the Waffen-SS stood Soviet armor of the 5th Guards Tank Army, which also began their advance toward the German lines. In total, the Soviets had about 500 tanks and self-propelled guns and began attacking the II SS Panzer Corps positions in two waves, with 430 tanks in the first echelon and 70 in the second. What followed was a climatic showdown in the fields and ridges in front of Prokhorovka as both sides fought to a standstill. Fighting was a fierce contest of attrition, and although the Waffen-SS showed great fortitude and determination, they were constantly hampered by stiff enemy resistance.

To counter the imbalance the Germans relied heavily on their Tigers and Panthers supported by well-armed panzergrenadiers, who continued with unabated ferocity to fight with courage and zeal. Since 1942 the Tiger had dominated the battlefield on the Eastern Front, and although by mid-1943 there were never enough available in sufficient numbers for offensive battles, they still played a key role. Again and again these armored monsters demonstrated their awesome killing power, playing a prominent role at Kursk against numerically superior Soviet armored forces.

The following morning of July 13, further fighting continued around Prokhorovka as the Soviet 10th Guards Mechanized Brigade and the 24th Guards Tank Brigade, supported by the 95th and 52nd Guards Rifle Division, launched a fierce attack against Totenkopf in order to deny it access along the road to Prokhorovka. Along the Psel River panzer units from the Leibstandarte's 1st SS Panzer Reconnaissance Battalion became heavily engaged in the fighting in support of the Totenkopf. Fighting in the area was brutal and unrelenting with panzergrenadiers embroiled in heavy contact with the enemy for long periods. Without any significant support, Waffen-SS troops were regularly exposed to heavier fire, which brought about a never-ending strain on them.

Flak troops rest in a field next to their Sd.Kfz.10/4 halftrack armed with a mounted 2cm flak gun. Antiaircraft defenses came into prominence from late 1941, as the Soviet Air Force started to inflict heavy casualties. By the time the Kursk offensive began both Heer and Waffen-SS mechanized formations were well equipped with flak guns to counter this threat.

A group of SS panzergrenadiers hitching a ride on a Pz.Kpfw.IV. By July 13, the Red Army had dealt the SS and the Heer panzer divisions a severe battering from which the German war machine would struggle to recover. The final nail in the coffin for the Wehrmacht came when Hitler decided to withdraw the Totenkopf, Leibstandarte, and Das Reich divisions from the Kursk battlefield.

A Waffen-SS MG42 crew with bipod extended go into action. They have dismounted from a VW Type 166 Schwimmwagen. These amphibious four-wheel drive off-roaders were used extensively throughout the war. The Type 166 was the most common mass-produced amphibious car to roll off the assembly lines in Germany.

An Sd.Kfz.251/3 radio vehicle advances through a field.

Advancing along a road is an Sd.Kfz.10/4. Mounted on the back of the halftrack is a 2cm flak gun. The vehicle is towing an Sd.Ah.51 ammunition trailer.

Pz.Kpfw.IIIs halted in a field. Initially the German armored attack at Kursk went well, with the panzers scoring sizable successes along some parts of the front.

As a result of heavy Russian resistance and firepower, the Totenkopf commanders were all too well aware that they would have to abandon their positions northwest of Prokhorovka and conduct their withdrawal toward the feature known as Hill 226.6, which was deemed more defensible to hold. By nightfall the Waffen-SS had withdrawn, in spite of Russian attempts to sever the route to the hill.

The withdrawal of the Waffen-SS was a clear indication that the situation in Army Group South was deteriorating. Army Group Center had already stagnated and was slowing siphoning off troops and armor needed elsewhere. This had put an ever-increasing strain on the south, and too much expectation on Hausser's men.

Elsewhere, in what became known as the "Prokhorovka Cauldron," the XLVIII Panzer Corps had halted, licking its wounds at the River Psel. The 3rd Panzer Division was now down to 50 tanks, and, in order to avoid total disintegration, the Grossdeutschland was moved up in support. The 11th Panzer Division, too, fared little better and also reported it only had about 50 battleworthy tanks remaining and was in no position to open an attack against the Soviets. Yet, in spite of the dire situation in which Army Group South found itself, the II SS Panzer Corps and III Panzer Corps were to continue their offensive operations, but for a limited period of time.

Destroyed Soviet tanks in a field. In spite of high losses, the Red Army fielded some two million men and over 5,000 tanks, an extremely potent array of military hardware.

Over the next two days the 7th and 19th Panzer Divisions continued their offensive toward Prokhorovka. To the west the Grossdeutschland with the 3rd Panzer Division counterattacked the Soviet 5th Guards and 10th Tank Corps, with some success. However, it was clear by the morning of July 14 that *Zitadelle* could not succeed. Even the II SS Panzer Corps was showing signs of significant wear and tear. The Leibstandarte, for instance, reported it only had 57 tanks and 28 assault guns left.

It was clear by July 15 that Army Group South was tactically in a most dangerous position, more so than it had ever faced before. The front was badly scarred and depleted and the bulk of its forces were holding a thin line with little to fight with. All across the salient savage battles had been fought. The stench of the fighting permeated every road, field, and street. Along the main road leading to Prokhorovka hundreds of fires burned and flickered as buildings and the charred remains of armored vehicles bore testimony to the determination of the Russians who had so ferociously denied their German foe. The German forces left at Kursk, now awaited their fate of either continuing a battle that was doomed, or being withdrawn to save their remaining men and equipment to fight another day.

The End

By July 13, it had become totally clear that the Soviets had finally ground down the Wehrmacht at Kursk and thrown its offensive timetable irreversibly off schedule. At Hitler's East Prussian headquarters, the "Wolf's Lair," the Führer was clearly disturbed by the setback and during a number of conferences he told his generals that he was thinking of calling off *Zitadelle* altogether. As further news from Kursk brought increasing gloom, Hitler

An early-production Tiger I rolls past a burning building. This tank belongs to the 505th Heavy Tank Battalion.

summoned both army group commanders, Manstein and Kluge, to the "Wolf's Lair." He told them that in view of reports of enemy landings on Sicily, where the Italians were not even attempting to fight, it was necessary to form new armies in Italy and the western Balkans. These forces, he said, must be found from the Eastern Front, so *Zitadelle* had to be halted. In other words, Hitler knew that if he continued with the offensive, the whole of Army Group Center would be destroyed.

For the first time in the war the Soviets had determinedly contested every foot of ground and were finally on an equal footing, and more. The German offensive at Kursk had dealt the Wehrmacht a severe battering and ended the largest tank battle in history. It was reported to Hitler's headquarters in East Prussia that the Germans had lost some 30 divisions, including seven panzer divisions. As many as 40,000 German troops were reported killed and missing. They had lost a staggering 1,614 tanks and self-propelled guns. The Red Army had suffered far bigger losses. Some 1.2 million Russian soldiers had been killed or wounded, but the Red Army was infinitely more capable of sustaining their losses than the Germans.

Yet, in view of these losses, Manstein appeared more optimistic than his Führer. The field marshal argued that his forces could still inflict terrible casualties on the Red Army's strategic reserves, and that with further perseverance, Army Group South could still attain its objectives. Hitler, however, remained adamant: *Zitadelle* would be cancelled. Instead, he said, his forces would turn their attention to a post-defensive phase of the Kursk battle in order to avoid losing more men and armor.

Much to Hitler's relief, stability once more returned, albeit temporarily, to the Eastern Front as exhausted Red Army forces refitted and resupplied. Despite the German failure at Kursk, Hitler and his commanders clung to the view that the fighting there had squeezed the Soviets of all their available resources. They ardently believed that the rest of the summer campaign could be devoted to a series of tactical solutions that would straighten out the front and prepare their defenses for the onset of the winter.

In southern Russia it was reported that a number of advanced units of Army Group South had tried their best to hold onto vital areas of ground in order to contain the overly extended front. During the last two weeks of July Army Group South had a total of 822,000 troops opposing an estimated 1,710,000 Russians. Here in the south commanders expressed their concerns at the situation conferences that the majority of units were seriously under strength and still further depleted by vehicles constantly being taken out for repair. This undoubtedly left a substantial lack of armor to support the troops on the front lines.

As a consequence Army Group South was forced to withdraw in order to prevent being cut off and perhaps suffer the same fate as the Sixth Army at Stalingrad. During the last week of July a report was received that a substantial amount of men and their equipment had begun a series of withdrawals. In the central and southern sectors of the Eastern Front Wehrmacht units were trying to desperately stop the Red Army from breaking through. But their strength had hemorrhaged during the *Zitadelle* offensive.

A Panther tank knocked out of action. An antitank round has clearly struck the 7.5cm barrel.

Aftermath

The reverberations caused by the defeat at Kursk meant that German forces in the south bore the brunt of the heaviest Soviet offensive drive to date. Both the Russian Voronezh and Steppe Fronts possessed massive local superiority against everything the Germans had on the battlefield, and this included their diminishing resources of tanks and assault guns.

The Panzerwaffe were now duty-bound to improvise with what they had at their disposal and to attempt to maintain themselves in the field, and in so doing they hoped to wear down the enemy's offensive capacity. But in the south where the weight of the Soviet effort was directed, Army Group South's line began breaking and threatened to rip wide open. Stiff defensive action was now the stratagem placed upon the Panzerwaffe, but they lacked sufficient reinforcements and the strength of their armored units dwindled steadily as they tried to hold back the Soviet juggernaut.

Littering the battlefield as two Russian soldiers pass by is the turret of a Pz.Kpfw.IV Ausf.H which has obviously suffered a catastrophic internal explosion most likely caused by a larger-caliber artillery round through the turret roof. The explosion has blown the superstructure and turret completely off the chassis. Note the small tactical number 624 painted on the turret *schürzen* armor.

A Marder III in a field, knocked out and abandoned. The high-top open compartment and thin armor made this tank destroyer vulnerable to both tank and antitank fire.

During the first uneasy weeks of August 1943 the First Panzer Army and Army Detachment Kempf fought to hold ground along the Donets River whilst the final battle of Kharkov played out.

Farther north near the battered town of Akhtyrka the Fourth Panzer Army was also fighting a frenzied battle of attrition. Along the whole Russian front massive Soviet artillery bombardments would sweep the German lines and inflict considerable casualties on both infantry and armored vehicles.

Throughout August and September the Panzerwaffe tried frantically to hold the receding front. With just over 1,000 panzers operating in southern Russia, the Germans were seriously under strength and still further depleted by vehicles being constantly taken

A Soviet light tank passes a totally destroyed Pz.Kpfw.IV. It is clear that the panzer suffered a catastrophic internal explosion; the crew probably never stood a chance.

A Russian tank burns following an internal explosion. The Red Army lost huge amounts of armor and men at Kursk, but where the Germans could not replace their losses, the Soviets were able to do so quickly and effectively.

out for repair. Along many areas of the front, high losses resulted from inadequate supplies less than the skill of the enemy.

Farther north the situation was just as dire. Both Army Group Center and Army Group North were trying desperately to stop the Soviets from breaking through. Replacements continued to trickle through to help bolster the understrength Panzerwaffe, but in truth, the average fresh recruit was not as well trained as his predecessors. Nevertheless, as with many panzermen, they were characterized by high morale and a determination to do their duty.

In almost three months since the defeat at Kursk Army Group Center and Army Group South had been pushed back an average distance of 150 miles across a 650-mile front. Despite heavy resistance in many sectors of the front, the Soviets lost no time in exploiting the fruits of victory and regaining as much territory as possible. In Army Group South where the front threatened to collapse under intense enemy pressure, frantic appeals to Hitler were

A Tiger on fire, destroyed by an internal explosion so disastrous that it has blown the turret clean off its mounting; part of its track can be seen lying next to the vehicle.

made by Field Marshal Manstein to withdraw his forces across the Dnieper River. What followed was a fighting withdrawal that degenerated into a race for possession of the river. Whilst the Panzer divisions covered the rear, the army group's columns withdrew to selected river crossing points at Cherkassy, Dniepropetrovsk, Kiev, Kanev, and Krmenchug, leaving behind a blasted wasteland.

The crossing of the Dnieper River before the battered and worn front disintegrated into total ruin was one of the major achievements in von Manstein's career. The Germans still believed they could stabilize the front, but Soviet numerical superiority was far too great. By trying to hold the eastern side of the Dnieper, Army Group South's and Army Group Center's strength had been almost irreversibly sapped.

The Panzerwaffe was now required to try and perform yet another reversal of Germany's fortunes in the East. In most areas of the front panzer crews were no longer to adopt any risky offensive tactics but to use a delaying and blocking strategy instead. As the third winter fast approached they hoped that the near-Arctic conditions would this time impede the onset of yet another Soviet offensive.

A knocked-out and abandoned Tiger Ferdinand tank hunter. These Ferdinands first saw combat at Kursk, where 89 were committed, the largest deployment of the vehicle during its service. During the offensive these heavy vehicles were plagued with problems such as susceptibility to mine damage and mechanical failure. Quite often, even with minor damage to their tracks or suspension, these vehicle had little hope of recovery, and crews were usually forced to destroy the vehicles to prevent a mostly intact tank from falling into enemy hands. Ferdinand units were deployed at company level, sometimes sub-divided into platoons, with infantry or tanks in support to protect the flanks and rear of the vehicles. With their powerful gun, they were often used along the front lines, where many were lost.

Further Reading

Buffetaut, Yves, *Casemate Illustrated: The 2nd SS Panzer Division Das Reich* (translated by H. McAdams), Casemate, Havertown, 2017

Fey, Will, *Armor Battles of the Waffen-SS 1943–45* (translated by H. Henschler), J. J. Fedorowicz Publishing, Manitoba, Winnipeg, 1990

Glantz, David M., *When Titans Clashed: How the Red Army Stopped Hitler*, University Press of Kansas, Lawrence, Kansas, 2015

Guderian, Heinz, *Panzer Leader*, E.P. Dutton & Co., New York, 1952

Healy, Mark, *Zitadelle: The German Offensive Against the Kursk Salient 4–17 July 1943*, The History Press, Stroud, 2016

Jentz, Thomas, *Panzer Truppen: 1943–1945*, Schiffer Publishing Ltd. (U.S.), Atglen, 1998

Lawrence, Christopher, *The Battle of Prokhorovka: The Tank Battle at Kursk, the Largest Clash of Armor in History*, Stackpole Books, Mechanicsburg, Pennsylvania, 2019

Lucas, James, *Das Reich: The Military Role of the 2nd SS Division 1941–45*, Arms & Armour Press, London, 1991

Mattson, Gregory L., *SS-Das Reich: The History of the Second SS Division 1941–45*, Amber Books, London, 2002

Mellenthin, F. W. von, *Panzer Battles: A Study of Employment of Armor in the Second World War*, University of Oklahoma Press, Oklahoma, 1956

Raus, Peter Erhard, *Panzer on the Eastern Front 1941–1945*, Greenhill, London, 2002

Toeppel, Roman, *Kursk 1943: The Greatest Battle of the Second World War*, Helion and Co., Solihull, 2018

Tucker-Jones, Anthony, *Images of War: Armoured Warfare and the Waffen-SS 1944–1945*, Pen and Sword, Barnsley, 2017

Williamson, Gordon, *The Waffen-SS*, Vols 1 & 2, Osprey, Oxford, 2003/4

A Waffen-SS column moving towards the front during the buildup of forces in the Kursk region in May and June 1943. The Waffen-SS units were commanded by SS-Obergruppenführer Paul Hausser, commander II SS Panzer Corps, which formed part of the Fourth Panzer Army.

Index

Belgorod, 11, 14, 54
Berghof, 35–36, 38, 43
Bletchley Park, 22
Bryansk Front (Russian), 31, 54
Butovo, 93
Bykovka, 95

Central Front (German), 14, 61
Central Front (Russian), 32, 61, 75
Cherkasskoe, 93
Cloessner, Erich-Heinrich (General), 57, 60

Das Reich, 51, 89, 95, 102, 107, 113
Defensive belts (Russian), 28, 51, 61, 102
Dnieper River, 124

German army
    505th Heavy Tank Battalion, 43, 56, 69, 76, 85
    Ninth Army (German), 36, 43, 49, 56–57, 60, 66, 75, 92
    Fourth Panzer Army, 11, 49, 88-89, 92–93, 123
    Army Detachment Kempf, 49, 88, 92–93, 102, 113, 123
    2nd Panzer Division, 52, 57, 76, 85
    3rd Panzer Division, 52, 89, 119-120
    4th Panzer Division, 52, 57
    5th Panzer Division, 53, 57
    6th Panzer Division, 9, 53, 89, 107
    7th Panzer Division, 53, 89
    8th Panzer Division, 53, 57
    9th Panzer Division, 57, 77
    11th Panzer Division, 49, 54, 89, 93, 107, 119
    12th Panzer Division, 54, 57
    17th Panzer Division, 49, 54, 89
    18th Panzer Division, 55, 57
    19th Panzer Division, 55, 89, 102, 120
    20th Panzer Division, 55, 57, 66, 69, 85
    II SS Panzer Corps, 13, 51, 89, 93, 95, 97, 105–7, 115, 119, 120
    III Panzer Corps, 49, 89, 113, 119
    XXIV Panzer Corps, 49, 89, 92
    XLI Panzer Corps, 43, 56, 57, 61, 66
    XLII Panzer Corps, 49, 89
    XLVI Panzer Corps, 43, 56, 57
    XLVII Panzer Corps, 43, 56, 57, 66
    XLVIII Panzer Corps, 49, 89, 93, 107, 119
    Panzer Corps, 13, 43, 49, 51, 56, 57, 61, 66, 89, 92, 93, 95, 97, 105–7, 113, 115, 119, 120
    393rd Assault Gun Detachment, 49
    905th Assault Gun Detachment, 49
    51st Panther Battalion, 49
    52nd Panther Battalion, 49
Grossdeutschland Division, 49, 51, 89, 93, 95, 98, 102, 104, 119, 120
Guderian, Heinz, General, 38

Hausser, Paul (SS-Obergruppenführer) 89, 95, 97, 105, 113, 119
Hitler, Adolf, 9, 13, 16, 22, 25, 35–36, 38, 40, 43, 51, 60, 83, 92, 95, 107, 113, 120–21, 124
Hoth, Herman, General, 89, 92–93
Hungarian divisions, 43

Kempf (Army Detachment), 49, 88–89, 92–93, 102, 113, 123
Kempf, Werner (General), 92
Kharkov, 11, 13, 14, 22, 35, 52, 53, 60, 92, 123
Kluge, Günther, von General, 57, 60, 121
Knobelsdorff, Schmidt von, General, 49, 89

Leibstandarte Adolf Hitler (Waffen-SS), 51, 89, 95, 97-98, 102, 107, 113, 116
Lucy spy ring, 22

Luftwaffe, 65, 89, 113

Manstein, Erich von (Field Marshal), 13–14, 89, 92, 121, 125
Model, Walter (General), 36, 43, 56–57, 60, 66, 69, 75, 77, 85–87

Nebelwerfer, 61, 65

Operation *Fall Blau* (Case Blue), 8
Operation *Little Saturn*, 11
Operation *Star*, 14
Operation *Zitadelle* (Citadel), 6, 34-36
Order 6, 36
Orel, 13–14, 22, 52, 54–55

Panther (Tank), 29, 38, 49, 51, 93, 102, 104, 115
Panzer.III (Pz.Kpfw.III), 43, 51, 66, 85, 91
Panzer.IV (Pz.Kpfw.IV), 58, 78-79, 91, 102
Panzerwaffe, 8, 14, 35–36, 51, 79, 87, 90, 98, 122-125
Pena River, 105
Postponement (Zitadelle), 38
PPSh-41 Machine Gun, 21
PPSh-43 Machine Gun, 21
Prokhorovka, 107, 113, 115, 119-120
Psel River, 119

Rotmistrov, Pavel (General), 33
Russian army
    1st Tank Army, 33
    2nd Tank Army, 32
    5th Guards Tank Army, 33, 115
    5th Guards Army, 33, 113
    5th Air Army, 33
    6th Guards Army, 33
    7th Guards Army, 33
    38th Army, 33
    40th Army, 33
    69th Army, 33
    2nd Air Army, 33
    3rd Army, 31
    50th Army, 31
    63rd Army, 31
    61st Army, 31
    11th Guards Army, 31
    1st Air Army, 31
    15th Air Army, 31
    13th Army, 32
    48th Army, 32
    60th Army, 32
    65th Army, 32
    70th Tank Army, 32
    16th Air Army, 32

Southern Front (German), 93
Stalin, Joseph, 22, 25

Steppe Front (Russian), 25, 28, 33, 122
Storozhevoe, 113
StuG.III (Sturmgeschütz.III), 49, 85
Sturmpanzer IV, 43

Tiger (Tank), 13, 26, 29, 43, 49, 51, 58, 69, 95, 98, 104, 113, 115
Tiger panzerjägers (Ferdinands), 43
T-34 (Tank), 26, 29, 85
Totenkopf, 16, 89, 95, 97, 102, 107, 113, 115, 119

Voronezh Front, 25, 28, 33, 39

Western Front (Russian), 31
Wiking Division (Waffen-SS), 49, 89
Wolf's Lair (Wolfschanze) 119
Weiss, Walter (General), 57, 60

Zeitzler, Kurt, 36
Zhukov, Georgi, Marshall, 22, 25
Zitadelle, 6, 34, 38, 43, 63, 107, 120-121